THE
Southern
MOUNTAIN
Kitchen
COOKBOOK

G.W. Mullins

 Light Of The Moon Publishing

ISBN: 978-1-958221-06-8
Printed in the United States of America

First Printing

Light Of The Moon has allowed this work to remain exactly as
the author intended, verbatim, without editorial input.

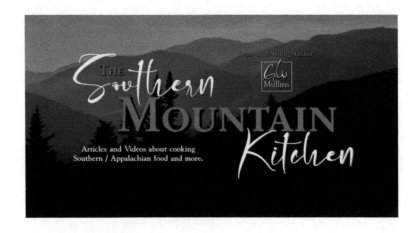

Visit G.W. Mullins for weekly cooking videos on The Southern Mountain Kitchen YouTube Channel:

https://www.youtube.com/channel/UCNvofqt_huM8Ey_rjx WsOhQ/videos

And the Southern Mountain Kitchen Blog:

https://thesouthernmountainkitchen.blogspot.com/

Southern and Mountain recipes hold an original flavor all their own. Often thought of as guilty pleasures, these foods are very down to earth and original. In this book, you will find the best of these recipes. From traditional post roast, to buttermilk biscuit, the recipes are all here. There is even a recipe for moonshine.

These are the wonderful foods you would have gotten when going to Grandma's house. This book will allow you to recreate those memories of the old days, with great food and family.

I have endeavored to combine the practical with the unusual, in order to provide an outstanding book of favorite foods that will be treasured and enjoyed by all. The book is all about family, friends and food.

Table Of Contents

Appetizers & Beverages 11

This & That 21

Soups Salads & Vegetables 27

Main Dishes & Casseroles 53

Meat, Poultry & Seafood 65

Pies, Pastry & Desserts 89

Breads & Rolls 115

Cakes, Cookies & Candy 133

Helpful Hints 172

Herbs & Spices 195

Baking Breads 198

Vegetables & Fruits 204

Microwave Hints 213

Calorie Counter 215

Cooking Terms 220

Appetizers and Beverages

Deviled Eggs

8 eggs, hard boiled, sliced in two lengthwise (remove yolks)
2 tbsp. butter
1/2 tsp. dry mustard
1/4 tsp. salt (more if desired)
3 tbsp. vinegar

Mix and beat butter, mustard, salt and vinegar together. Add mashed yolks and mix well. If mixture is dry, add enough mayonnaise to make a creamy mixture. Fill eggs halves with mixture and sprinkle with paprika.

Pickled Walnuts

Use about 100 walnuts or butternuts. Prick each with a needle well through, hold with cloth to avoid staining hands. Soak in salt water (1 ½ pints salt to 1 gallon of water) for 2 to 3 days changing the salt water each day. Then let stand for 3 days; drain and expose to sun for 3 days. After this pack in jars and cover with a gallon of vinegar that has been boiled with 1 cup sugar, 3 dozen cloves, 1 ½ dozen pepper corns, and a dozen blades of mace. Pour over walnuts while scalding hot. In three days, draw off vinegar, boil it, and pour over walnuts while hot. After 3 days repeat the last step. They will be ready to eat in one month. They will keep for a year.

Clover Tea

If Gathered: Gather when full grown, and dry at room temperature. When thoroughly dry grind into very fine particles, and seal in jars. This will help it to retain flavor.

If you are unable to do this you can find Clover Tea at your local grocery store.

Use 1 tsp. to each cup of boiling water. Brew in a cup or a teapot (as you would other teas), and sweeten with honey.

Parsnip Wine

For the right flavor the parsnips have to be taken out of the ground in February. If you are unable to do this you can find parsnips at the grocery store.
1-quart grated parsnips
1-gallon boiling water
2 1/2 lb. white sugar
1/4 teacup liquid yeast

How to make liquid yeast: Add warm water to yeast to liquefy the yeast.

Put grated parsnips in a stoneware jar, and pour boiling water over them. Set jar on the back of the stove where it will keep hot, but will not boil. Leave it there 4 hours, then strain. Wash jar, then return the liquid to it. Add the sugar, and stir until dissolved. When it is lukewarm add the yeast. Let stand until seasoned (about 2 weeks or until fermentation stops).

Home Brew

5-gallon crock or wooden keg
1 quart of store-bought red top malt
4 gallons of water
5 lbs. of sugar
2 small cakes of yeast

Heat about a 1/3 of the water from above. In the crock stir the sugar and malt with the heated water until it has dissolved. Cool it down with the cooler water to a milk warm temperature. Add the 2 cakes of yeast, and keep in a warm place. It foams and works about 3 days. Then it stops and the foam goes down and it's ready to bottle.

Moonshine

In making "Mountain Dew" or "White Lightning" the first step is to convert the starch of the grain into sugar. (Commercials distillers use malt.) This is done by "sprouting" the corn. Shelled, whole corn is covered with warm water in a container with a hole in the bottom. Place a hot cloth over it. Add warm water from time to time at it drains. Keep in a warm place for about 3 days or until corn has 2-inch sprouts. Dry it and grind it into meal. Make mush (or mash) with boiling water. Add rye mash that has been made the same way, if you have it.
Yeast (½ lb. per 50 gallons of mash) may be added to speed up the fermentation if you have it. Without it, 10 or more days will be required instead of about 4 days. In either case, it must be kept warm.

When the mash gets through "working" or bubbling up and settles down, it is then ready to run. At this stage, the mash has been converted into carbonic acid and alcohol. It is called "wash" or beer and it is <u>sour</u>.

The "cooker" consists of two main parts, mainly the top and the bottom. After the mash is put inside, the top is pasted on with "red dog chop" or some other paste. This is so that if the fire is too hot and the pressure builds up, the top will blow off preventing an explosion which might wreck the still.

In the top of the cooker a copper pipe, or "arm" projects over to one side and tapers down a 4- or 5-inch diameter to a same diameter as the "worm" (1" or 1 ¼")

To make the "worm", a 20-foot copper pipe is filled with sand, the ends are stopped up, and it is wrapped around a fence post. The sand prevents "kinking" of the pipe. The spiral or coil, called the worm, is then cleaned and attached firmly to the end of the arm in such a way that it is down inside a barrel. The barrel will be kept full of cold, running water. If the water runs in the top and out an opening at the bottom, it can circulate better.

A fire under the cooker causes the spirit to rise in vapor along with the steam. It goes into the arm and then into the "worm" where the cold water causes condensation. This is collected at the end in a container.

The first run off, or "singling", is weak and impure and must be redistilled to rid it of water and rank oils.
For the second run off, or the "doublings", the cooker is cleaned out and the "singlings", along with some water, is heated and run through again.

The first quart will be far too strong (about 200 proof) and toward the last it will be weak (about 10 proof). The skill is in the mixing to make it 100 proof.

If a tablespoon of the liquid does not "flash" or burn when thrown on the fire, there is not enough alcohol left to bother running any more.

To test for the right proof, a small glass vial is used. When the small bubbles rise properly after the vial is tilted and when they set half above and half below the top of the liquid, then it is the right proof. The liquor is then filtered through charcoal and is ready for consumption. This is just one way to make moonshine.

Salmon Patties

1 (15.5oz.) can Alaska salmon
3 slices bread (torn into small pieces)
1/3 cup minced onion
1/4 cup milk
2 eggs
2 tsp. minced parsley
1 tablespoon lemon juice
1/4 tsp. salt
1/4 tsp. dill
Dash pepper
2 tbsp. oil and flour

Drain the salmon, reserving 2 tbsp. of the liquid. Combine the salmon with the bread pieces, onion, milk, eggs, parsley, salt, dill, and pepper; mix thoroughly. Shape into 6 patties and coat each with flour lightly. Pan-fry on both sides in oil until golden brown.

Sausage Balls

1 lb. hot sausage (at room temperature)
10oz. extra-sharp cheese (grated)
3 cups Biscuit mix

Mix the Biscuit with the grated cheese, and then add the sausage. Blend thoroughly. Shape into small balls, and freeze on cookie sheet. Store them in a plastic bag in the freezer. Place the frozen balls on a greased cookie sheet. Bake at 300 degrees for 35 to 45 minutes. Serve hot. This makes about 4 dozen sausage balls.

Crab Dip

1 – 6.5oz. can crab meat
1/4 cup lemon juice
2 – 3oz. packages cream cheese (softened)
1/4 cup cream
1/4 cup mayonnaise
1/2 clove of garlic (crushed)
1 tsp. minced onions
1/2 tsp. chives
Salt to taste
1/8 tsp. Worcestershire sauce
2 drops of Tabasco sauce

Marinate the crab meat in the lemon juice for 1 hour; then drain. Combine the cream cheese and cream in a mixer bowl, and mix until smooth. Beat in the mayonnaise, and then add the garlic, onions, chives, and salt. Mix thoroughly. Fold the crab meat into this sauce. Add the Worcestershire sauce and the Tabasco sauce. It can be served hot or cold. This recipe will make about 20 servings.

Hot Pepper Cheese Ball

1 – 8oz. package cream cheese (softened)
1/4 lb. Cheddar cheese (grated)
1/4 lb. extra sharp cheese (grated)
1/4 lb. hot pepper cheese (grated)
1/4 tsp. onion salt
1/4 tsp. garlic salt

2 tbsp. salad dressing
1 tablespoon Worcestershire sauce
Chopped nuts

Combine all the ingredients, except the nuts, in a bowl, and blend thoroughly. Form this into a ball and refrigerate overnight. Roll in nuts and serve with crackers.

Wassail

2 quarts apple cider
2 cups orange juice
1 cup lemon juice
5 cups pineapple juice
1 stick cinnamon
1 tsp. whole cloves
Sugar or honey to taste
Orange Slices

Combine all the ingredients together except the orange slices in a large saucepan. Simmer slowly for 1 hour or longer. <u>Do not boil.</u> Strain before serving, and garnish with the orange slices.

Fresh Holiday Eggnog

1 dozen eggs (separated)
1 1/2 cups sugar
4 cups milk
1 cup whipping cream (whipped)
1/4 cup Brandy
1/4 cup light rum
1/2 tsp. vanilla extract
1/2 tsp. ground nutmeg

Beat the egg yolks in a bowl until they are smooth. Combine the egg yolks and the sugar in top of a double boiler over hot water. Stir in the milk gradually. Cook it, stirring constantly, until the mixture coats a spoon. Remove from the heat, and refrigerate until chilled. Beat the eggs whites until stiff peaks form. Fold the egg whites and whipped cream into the chilled egg yolk mixture. Then stir in the Brandy and rum. Chill for several hours to blend the flavors. Stir in the vanilla just before serving; sprinkle with nutmeg.

This recipe can make twenty-four 1/2 cup servings.

Deviled Eggs 2

Halve hard boiled eggs, lengthwise, and remove the yolks. Smash the yolks with 1/4 cup mayonnaise, 1 tsp. vinegar, 1 tsp. prepared mustard, 1/8 tsp. salt, and a dash of pepper. Refill the white halves with the yolk mixture.

Cheese Scallop

Soak 1 cup of dry bread crumbs in fresh milk. Beat in 3 eggs, and add 1 tablespoon butter and ½ lb. grated cheese. Arrange in iron skillet or baking dish. Strew with more bread crumbs and bake at 350 degrees for 25 minutes.

Deviled Eggs 3

6 hard-boiled eggs cut in half lengthwise
3 tbsp. dairy sour cream
2 tsp. cider (vinegar)
1 tsp. prepared mustard

1/4 tsp. salt
Mash egg yolks and add the other ingredients. Mix thoroughly. Fill the egg whites with the mixture, and store in refrigerator until ready to serve.

This and That

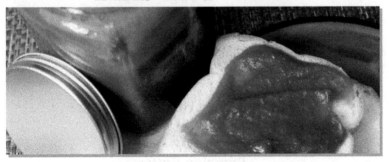

Pickled Eggs

1 dozen eggs (hard boiled and peeled)
3 cups distilled white vinegar
1/4 cup pickling spice
1/4 cup sugar
2 tsp kosher salt
2 cans whole beets (drained reserve 1 cup of juice)
1 jar pearl onions (drained)

In a medium sauce pan combine vinegar, pickling spice, beet juice, sugar and salt. Bring to a boil, then reduce heat to low and simmer for 5 minutes.

In a large glass sealable jar, add one can of drained beets, half the pearl onions, hard boiled eggs, second can of drained beets and remaining pearl onions.

Fill the jar with the pickling mix, ensuring to get all of the spices in the jar. You can add more vinegar if needed to top off. Seal the jar, shake well and let cool on the counter. Refrigerate for at least ten days.

Eggs are fully pickled after 10 days.

Pumpkin Butter

Yield: 5 - 1/2-pint jars

1 (29 ounce) can pumpkin puree
3/4 cup apple juice
2 tsp. ground ginger
1/2 tsp. ground cloves
1 1/2 cups white sugar
2 tsp. ground cinnamon

1 tsp. ground nutmeg

Combine pumpkin, apple juice, spices, and sugar in a large saucepan; stir well. Bring mixture to a boil. Reduce heat, and simmer for 30 minutes or until thickened. Stir frequently.

Transfer to sterile containers and chill in the refrigerator until serving.

Hominy Grits

1 cup hominy grits
1 tsp. salt
5 cups boiling water

Cook slowly, 25 to 30 minutes, stirring frequently. Serve with gravy or with butter or with cream and sugar. Chill the leftovers; slice and fry in butter until golden brown.

Delicious Mayonnaise

3 eggs well beaten, add 1/2 cup sugar with 1/2 tsp. mustard. 1 cup of cream, 1/2 cup of vinegar, add vinegar very slowly.

Cook in double boiler until thick. Do not boil. Add ½ tsp. salt when mixture is cool. 1 pint dressing.

Gooseberry Catsup

Boil 8 pounds of almost ripe gooseberries with 4 pounds brown sugar and one pint of vinegar for 3 or 4 hours. Add 2 ounces each of crumbled cinnamon and cloves tied in a cloth bag.

Boil 10 minutes more. Put in jars or bottles and seal.

Peach-Plum Jam

Wash, peel, and pit 4 cups peaches and 5 cups red plums. Cut fruit into small pieces, and place in a large kettle. Add 8 cups sugar and one thinly sliced lemon, stirring well into mix. Boil rapidly, stirring constantly until jellying point is reached, or until thick. Remove from heat; skim and stir alternately for 5 minutes. Ladle into hot jars and seal. This will yield 12 half pints.

Apple Butter

Cook slowly for 30 minutes 8 cups of apples, 5 cups sugar, ½ cup vinegar, ½ pound red cinnamon candy. Put in hot, sterile jars and seal.

Ham Curing

This recipe is enough to cure 8 hams.
Rub each ham well with a mixture of 8 quarts of salt, 16 tbsp. of black pepper, and 16 tbsp. of white sugar. Put some mixture into the shank bone. Wrap in brown paper and place in cloth bag. Hang with shank facing down.

Red Beet Eggs

2 - 1 lb. cans small whole beets
1 cup vinegar
½ cup sugar
1 tsp. salt
Salad Greens
6 eggs (hard boiled, shelled)

Drain beets, but save the liquid. Place the beets in a 1 ½ quart jar. Measure reserved liquid. Add water to have 1 cup liquid if not enough. In small sauce pan, combine beet liquid, vinegar, sugar, and salt. Bring to a boil, stirring. Pour over beets, then refrigerate tightly covered for 24 hours. Next day remove beets from the jar and put the eggs in the jar. Refrigerate covered 24 hours. Also refrigerate beets covered. To serve, drain eggs, halve lengthwise. Slice beets. Arrange eggs on the salad greens along with sliced beets.

Soups, Salads, and
Vegetables

Southern Green Beans with Ham Hocks

2 lbs. green beans (fresh or frozen)
2 cups water
3 smoked ham hocks
1 yellow onion (cut into small pieces)
4 garlic cloves (minced)
1 tsp. salt
1 tsp. pepper

Combine all ingredients in a 6-quart crock pot. Cover, set on low for six hours.

Stir after 3 hours and continue to cook until ham hocks and green beans are tender.

Pan Fried Potatoes and Onions

2 lbs. russet potatoes (washed and cut into slices)
1 medium yellow onion (grated or finely sliced)
1/4 cup olive oil
1/2 tsp. each, salt & pepper
1/2 tsp. garlic powder
1/2 tsp. paprika

Grate a medium yellow or white onion, then wash and cut potatoes. Some people do leave on the skins, it is your choice.

Heat the cooking oil in a large frying pan, skillet, or cast-iron skillet over medium heat.

Add the grated onions, cut potatoes, and seasoning (salt, pepper, paprika, and garlic powder).

Stir the ingredients together, then spread them in an even layer over the bottom of your pan. Cover lid and cook for 15 minutes, or more until golden brown.

After the 15 minutes uncover and stir the potatoes and onions. Leave uncovered to finish for about 10 minutes, or until your potatoes are fork-tender.

Remove from heat after cooking and serve immediately.

Choice Chicken Salad

6 eggs (hard boiled)
½ cup chopped pickle
1 5lb. or 6lb. chicken (cooked and chopped)
Nuts if desired

Mix contents together well. Add special dressing listed below.

Special Dressing for Chicken Salad

1 ½ cups sugar
½ tsp. mustard
½ tsp. salt
1 tablespoon flour
2 beaten eggs
1 cup sweet milk
1 cup vinegar
Dash of red pepper

Mix dry ingredients and add beaten eggs, milk and vinegar. Cook until thick or the desired consistency is reached.

Oven Baked Potato Wedges

4 large washed potatoes
1/2 cup of regular olive oil
1 tbsp. of garlic powder
1 tbsp. of smoked paprika
1 tbsp of dried Italian herbs
1/2 cup of parmesan cheese
1 tsp. of salt
fresh black pepper

Preheat oven to 400 degrees. Slice potatoes into wedges and coat them with olive oil. Spread over top, garlic, smoked paprika, mixed Italian herbs, salt, pepper and parmesan cheese. Stir the potatoes to coat. Lay potatoes flat over a baking sheet. Bake until golden and tender, about 50 minutes approx.

Crab Salad (Seafood Salad)

1 lb. imitation crab meat
1 Shallot minced (or reg. onion)
1/2 cup mayonnaise
1/2 cup celery minced
1/2 tsp. paprika
1/2 tsp. dill
1/4 tsp. salt
1/4 tsp. black pepper

In a large bowl add all the ingredients together, gently stirring until well coated. Refrigerate for an hour before serving.

Mashed Potato Pancakes

2 cups mashed potatoes
1-2 eggs
1/4 cup flour
Salt to taste
Pepper to taste
Garlic to taste
chopped onion (optional)
chives (optional)
cheese (optional)
oil or Crisco, for frying

Add all ingredients into a medium bowl and mix until combined. Heat a cast iron skillet or pan with enough oil to coat bottom. When hot, add potato mixture as you would with a pancake, and spread it into a circle whatever size you like. Then, cook for several minutes on each side until both are golden brown. All to cool for 5 minutes before eating.

Meatball Parmesan

1/2 cup dry breadcrumbs or 4 slices stale white bread
2 tbsp. milk or buttermilk
3 eggs lightly beaten
1 tbsp. salt
1/4 tsp. ground black pepper
1/2 cup grated Parmesan cheese divided
1 1/2 tsp. dried parsley
1 1/2 tsp. dried basil
1/2 tsp. dried oregano
1 1/2 lbs. ground chuck or a blend of Italian sausage and ground chuck
2 cups spaghetti or marinara sauce

1/2 lbs. fresh mozzarella cut into 2-inch pieces

Adjust oven rack to middle position and heat oven to 400°F. Cover a large baking sheet with aluminum foil and spray the foil with nonstick cooking spray.

Place the breadcrumbs or cut pieces of bread and milk in a large mixing bowl and stir until breadcrumbs are coated.

Set aside until liquid is almost absorbed. Add eggs, salt, pepper, Parmesan, parsley, basil, oregano to the breadcrumbs/milk mixture. Add ground meat and mix, until incorporated, and form into 3-inch balls.

Place the balls on the prepared baking sheet and bake at 400 degrees for 30 minutes or until cooked through.

Set the oven to 375°F, and prepare to make sauce. Coat a large skillet (that can be placed in the oven) with canola oil or spray with cooking spray.

Place 1-cup of sauce in the skillet and cover with a third of the grated Parmesan. Place the meatballs in the skillet. Pour the remaining sauce over the meatballs and add another third of the grated Parmesan.

Transfer skillet to the oven and bake at 375°F for 20-30 minutes or until sauce is bubbly. Top each meatball with the mozzarella cheese and the remaining Parmesan. Cook just until the cheese is melted.

Allow to cool 5-10 minutes before serving.

Cole Slaw

1 tbsp. sugar
2 tsp. mayonnaise
1/4 tsp. salt
few grains pepper
2 tsp. melted butter
1 egg
3/4 cup light cream
1/4 cup vinegar
paprika
4 cups shredded cabbage

Combine sugar, mayonnaise, salt and pepper. Beat egg, add melted butter and cream. Mix well. Add vinegar very slowly, cook over hot water, stirring all the while until mixture thickens. Chill. Toss dressing with shredded cabbage. Sprinkle with paprika.

Cottage Cole Slaw

1/2 cup cottage cheese
1/2 cup mayonnaise
3 tbsp. vinegar
1 1/2 tsp. onion juice
6 cups fine shredded cabbage
3/4 tsp. salt
1/2 tsp. pepper
1 tsp. caraway seed (optional)
1/2 chopped medium green pepper
2 cups diced apples

Combine cottage cheese, mayonnaise. Add vinegar, onion juice, seasonings, and caraway seed. Combine dressing with cabbage, apples and green pepper. Place in large bowl lined with cabbage leaves. Garnish with cottage cheese and green pepper. Chill. Makes 8-10 servings.

Butter Bean Salad

1 cup cooked butter beans
1/3 cup chopped celery
3 green onions, chopped
2 hard cooked sliced eggs
4 tsp. chopped pimiento
4 tsp. chopped parsley
4 tsp. chopped green pepper
French dressing

Drain beans. Chill all ingredients and combine. Toss with generous amount of French dressing. Serve on crisp lettuce leaves.

Cranberry Salad

2 cups cranberries
1 orange
1 1/2 cups sugar
1/2 cup chopped nuts
1/2 cup chopped celery
1 package strawberry Jell-O

Dissolve Jell-o in 1/4 cup of hot water. Grind cranberries, orange, nuts and celery in meat grinder. Add sugar, stir, let set at least one hour. Add cooled Jell-o and serve when set. Whipped cream may be used as topping if desired.

Cranberry Sauce

2 cups fresh cranberries
1/2 cup water
3/4 cup sugar

Cook cranberries and water until tender, about 2 minutes. Mash with a potato masher. Add the ¾ cup of sugar. Cook 1 minute longer. Chill.

Kraut Salad

1 cup drained kraut
1 cup diced celery
1/2 cup diced peppers
1/2 cup chopped onions
1 1/4 cup sugar
1/4 cup cooking oil
1/4 cup vinegar
1/4 tsp. salt

Mix ingredients for dressing. Chill. Mix with salad ingredients. Chill and serve.

Mountaineer Salad

Small head of cabbage (Grated or sliced)
1/2 cup cooked peanuts
1 cup crushed pineapple
2 cups small marshmallows

Combine ingredients and add mayonnaise as desired just before serving.

Lettuce and Onion Salad

2 tsp. melted bacon grease
2 tbsp. vinegar
1 tablespoon sugar
1 1/2 quarts shredded lettuce
3 chopped green onions

Combine the grease, vinegar, and sugar to boiling point and pour over the lettuce, onions. Add salt and pepper to taste. Toss and then it's ready to serve.

Potato Salad Dressing

Beat 3 eggs with 1/2 cup sugar and 1/2 cup vinegar, add 2 tsp. butter, one tsp. dry mustard, 1/2 tsp. salt and pepper to taste. Cook in a double boiler or over low heat until thick. If it gets too thick, thin it with some cream.

Mustard Beans for Canning

Cook together until tender: 1-gallon green beans, 1/2-gallon small onions, 1/2-gallon cucumbers, 1/2 cup salt, 1 cup sugar, 1 quart vinegar, in 1 quart of water. Add 2 tsp. mixed spices and 1 cup flour dissolved in water. Add 1 box prepared mustard. Cook 5 minutes, and store in sterile jars.

Sweet Pickle Sticks

3 3/4 cups vinegar
3 tbsp. salt
4 1/2 tsp. turmeric
3 cups sugar

4 1/2 tsp. celery seed
3/4 tsp. mustard seed

Use fresh, firm, medium cucumbers. Wash and cut into quarters. Pour boiling water over them and let stand overnight. Next morning, pack solidly into clean jars. Make pickling solution, boil 5 minutes, and pour hot solution over cucumbers. Put on lids and seal. Fills 6-pint jars.

Lime Pickles

7 cups sliced cucumbers
2 gallons water
2 cups dry lime

Mix the lime, water and cucumbers in container. Let stand for 24 hours. Then wash at least 5 times in cold water, and cover with fresh water. Let stand for 3 hours. Drain and add 1/2-gallon vinegar minus one cup, 4 cups sugar and 1 tablespoon salt. Mix well. Add cucumbers and let stand for another 24 hours. Heat for 35 minutes, place in jars and seal.

Special Pickles

Wash and cut (lengthwise) some fresh cucumbers. Pack into sterilized quart jars. To each quart add 2 tsp. of salt and 1 tsp. of alum (powdered). Fill jars with vinegar seal. Let stand 3 or 4 weeks. Drain off brine and add 2 cups white sugar and 2 tbsp. of pickling spice in a little cloth bag and seal.

Watermelon Rind Pickles

2 quarts diced watermelon rind
1 tsp. lime juice
2 cups sugar
1 cup vinegar
10 drops oil of cinnamon
10 drops oil of cloves

Add rind and lime juice to quart of water and soak overnight. Rinse rind, drain and cook in water for about an hour or until tender. Then mix sugar, vinegar, oil, and add these to the rind. Simmer mixture for 10 minutes and set aside for one night. Drain. Fill pickle jars with mixture. Boil one quart vinegar until clear and thick and add this to rind already in jars and seal.

Green Tomato Pickles

Chop a half peck of tomatoes, 3 onions, a gill of horse-radish, 3 green peppers; put in a sieve and drain dry. Salt in layers and let stand overnight. Drain them. Scald vinegar and pour over it; let stand two to three days then drain again. Mix quart of vinegar, one tablespoon of black pepper, the same of allspice, 3 ounces of ground cloves, three ounces of mustard, and a gill of mustard seed. Bring to a boil, and pour over the pickles and let stand.

Pickled Beans

Mix 2/3 cup of lemon juice, 1/2 cup oil, 2 tsp. salt and pepper, 1 tsp. dry mustard, 1/2 cup pearl onions. Add to 1lb. green beans (cooked briefly) in a crock. Let stand 4 days.

Pepper Hash

Wash, remove seeds, and chop 1 dozen sweet red peppers, 1 dozen sweet green peppers, 1 dozen small green onions. Add 3 tsp. salt and cook slowly for 10 minutes. Drain and add 4 cups mild vinegar and 1 cup brown sugar. Bring to boiling point, put in sterile jars and seal.

Cucumber Pickles

Wash 6 pounds of pickling cucumbers, 2/3 cup green pepper (chopped), 1 1/2 cup celery (chopped), and 6 medium onions (sliced). Blend 1/4 cup of prepared mustard with 2/3 cup vinegar. Then add 4 cups vinegar along with 1/2 cup of salt, 3 1/2 cups sugar, 2 tbsp. mustard seed, 1/2 tsp. turmeric, 1/2 tsp. whole cloves, 3 tbsp. celery seed, and 1 1/2 tsp. of powdered alum. Cover and bring to a boil. Reduce to a simmer and begin packing into hot, sterilized jars and seal. This makes about 9 pints.

Bread and Butter Pickles

Use 4 quarts medium-sized, sliced cucumbers. Make sure they are not seedy and that they are sliced thin, but do not peel the cucumbers. Add 6 medium white onions (sliced thin), 2 green peppers (chopped), 3 whole garlic cloves, and add 1/3 cup salt. Mix together thoroughly. Let stand for 4 hours in covered container with cracked ice, and then drain well. Combine 5 cups sugar, 1 1/2 tsp. turmeric, 1 1/2 tsp. celery seed, 2 tbsp. mustard seed, and 3 cups vinegar. Pour this over the cucumber mixture. Heat just to the boiling point, and seal at once in hot sterilized jars.

Red and Green Mix It

4 small zucchini squash
4 tomatoes
4 bell peppers
4 onions
1 eggplant
1 clove garlic
2 tbsp. olive oil
3 tbsp. lemon juice
2 tsp. sugar
Salt and pepper to taste

Peel and slice the zucchini, tomatoes, onions, and eggplant.
Seed and quarter peppers. Mince the garlic. Heat olive oil
in large pot, and add the vegetables and seasonings in
layers. Cook slowly for 50 to 60 minutes. Stir gently
occasionally. It can be served hot or cold. This recipe
serves 6 to 8.

Frozen Fruit Salad

2 cups canned fruit
1 tsp. gelatin
3 tbsp. fruit juice
1/2 cup mayonnaise
2/3 cup whipped cream
Salt, paprika, lettuce, powdered sugar, and dressing
Soak the gelatin in the fruit juice, then take this and
dissolve it over hot water. Add slowly to mayonnaise. Stir
in the fruit and use the other ingredients to season to taste.
Freeze for best results. This will serve 6.

Mountaineer Hash

Cook 1 medium chopped onion, 1 medium chopped pepper, and 3 tbsp. butter together until onion is yellow. Add 1 lb. ground beef and sauté until mixture falls apart. Add 2 cups canned tomatoes, 1 tsp. chili powder, 1/4 tsp. pepper, 1/2 cup uncooked rice, and 1 tsp. salt. Mix and poor into greased baking dish. Bake at 350 degrees for 45 minutes.

Creamy Cabbage

8 cups shredded cabbage
1 cup milk
1 tsp. salt
1 tsp. celery seed
2 eggs (beaten)
2 tbsp. melted butter
1/4 tsp. pepper

Cover the cabbage with cold water and let stand for about 1 hour. Drain and put in large sauce pan. Cover with boiling water. Simmer uncovered for 7 minutes. Do not overcook. Combine the remaining ingredients and fold in the cabbage. Turn into buttered baking dish and bake for 30 minutes at 375 degrees.

Leather Britches Beans

Wash and drain a batch of firm green beans. Remove ends and strings. Use a large darning needle with heavy white thread through the pod near the middle of each pushing the along the thread so that they are about 1/4" apart. Hang up the strings of beans in a warm, well-ventilated place to dry. They will shrivel and turn a greenish gray. To cook in the winter time, cover with water, and parboil slowly for half an hour. Drain again. Cook slowly with ham hock or salt pork until tender. Serve with cornbread.

Baked Beats

Dice 6 or 8 beets and put in a casserole dish. Mix 2 tsp. flour, 1/2 cup sugar, 1/2 tsp. salt, 1/4 cup water, 1/2 cup vinegar, and 1 tablespoon butter. Pour over beats. Bake in bean pot at 350 degrees for 1 hour.

Dandelion Greens

The greens can be used until they bloom. Pick over carefully, and wash several times, changing water each time. Put them in boiling water with a piece of salt pork, and boil for 1 hour. Drain well. Then put them in another batch of salted boiling water for 2 hours. When well done and tender, turn into colander and drain.

Party Peas

1 lb. fresh peas (or 1 box of frozen peas)
2 hard-boiled eggs
Medium white sauce
1/2 cup cracker crumbs
1/4 cup of mushrooms

Cook peas in salted water. Add peas to white sauce. Add chopped boiled eggs and mushrooms. Place in baking dish, spread with crushed cracker crumbs. Bake in 325–350-degree oven until brown.

Scalloped Potatoes

6 medium white potatoes
Salt and pepper to taste
1 cup milk
Lump of butter
a little flour

Wash, pare, and slice thin the raw potatoes. Arrange in layers in a greased baking dish. Season each layer with salt, pepper, and dust lightly with flour. Dot this with butter. After the potatoes have been used add enough milk to come within 1" of the top of the potatoes. Bake it for 1 hour at 350 degrees.

Easy Corn Pudding

2 cups fresh corn
2 tsp. sugar
1 1/2 tsp. salt
1/8 tsp. pepper
3 eggs (slightly beaten)
2 tbsp. butter
2 cups milk

Combine the corn, sugar, salt, and pepper. Add the eggs and mix. Add the butter to the milk, then heat until butter is melted. Blend the milk with the corn and egg. Put into baking dish, and bake at 325 degrees for 1 hour or until knife comes out clean.

Fried Sweet Potatoes

Peel and cut sweet potatoes. Put oil in skillet, keep turning potatoes. When almost done, add 3 to 4 tsps. brown sugar and 3/4 cup sweet milk. Place on low heat, let simmer until done. Best when served hot.

Navy Beans

Wash the navy beans, and pick out the old ones. Put the good ones in a large pan with enough cold water to cover about 1". Boil at medium heat for one hour. (Check to make sure the water continues to cover the beans, add if needed.) One-half hour after starting boiling, put 5 cups cold water in another pan and steak of fat. Turn on at medium heat and boil. After the beans have cooked the first hour, pour the remaining water off (should be very little) and add the meat and water mixture. Continue to boil at medium heat for almost another hour. In the last ten minutes, add salt. Turn the heat down and let simmer until serving, stirring occasionally.

Potato Soup

2 (10.5oz.) cans of chicken consommé
1 soup can of water
2 cups diced potatoes
2 scallions, chopped
1 soup can of milk
1 tsp. Worcestershire sauce
1/2 cup sour cream

Combine the consommé with the water, potatoes, and scallions in a large saucepan; bring this to a boil. Reduce

the heat and let simmer until potatoes are tender, for about 12 minutes. Blend until smooth in a blender and return to a saucepan. Stir in the milk and Worcestershire sauce; heat. Stir in the sour cream. This can be eaten hot or cold.
This recipe makes 4 to 6 servings.

Stuffed Peppers

3/4 cup cooked macaroni
6 medium green peppers
1 lb. ground beef
1 1/4 cup tomato soup (or 1 can)
1 egg (beaten)
1/2 tsp. salt
1/4 tsp. pepper
2 tbsp. ketchup
2 tbsp. chopped onion

Cook macaroni in 2 quarts boiling water and 1 tsp. salt. Blanch peppers 3 to 5 minutes, after removing seeds. Combine meat and soup and the rest of the unused ingredients. Fill the peppers with the mixture and replace cap of the pepper. Bake at 350 degrees for 30-35 minutes. Top each pepper with a little of the soup and bake 10 minutes or until tender.

Chow Chow

1-peck green tomatoes
2 heads cabbage
12 onions
6 green peppers
6 red peppers
4 banana peppers (hot!)

9 cups vinegar
6 cups sugar
2 tbsp. white mustard seed
2 tbsp. turmeric
1 tablespoon salt

Put the tomatoes, cabbage, onions, and peppers through a food processor and let drain overnight.
Add the vinegar, sugar, mustard seed, turmeric, and salt.
Cook at medium heat for 30 minutes and seal in sterilized jars.

This will make 12 to 16 pints.

Macaroni Salad

1 cup mayonnaise
2 tbsp. cider vinegar
1 tablespoon prepared mustard
1 tsp. sugar
1 tsp. salt
1/4 tsp. pepper
8oz. box elbow macaroni (cooked and drained)
1 cup celery (sliced)
1 large green or red pepper
1 small onion (chopped)
In a large bowl combine the mayonnaise, vinegar, mustard, sugar, salt, and pepper. Mix thoroughly. Add the macaroni, celery, green pepper, and onion. Mix thoroughly again.
Cover and chill.

This makes about 8 to 10 servings.

Sea Leg Delight

1/2 pounds sea legs
1/4 cup celery
1/2 cup mayonnaise
16 oz. box elbow macaroni

In a serving bowl break up the sea legs in small pieces and set aside. Chop the celery. Boil the macaroni and drain. Add all the ingredients together and blend with spoon, salt to taste, and keep refrigerated until ready to serve. This recipe makes about 4 to 6 servings.

Thanksgiving Yams with Topping

4 or 5 medium sized yams
1 cup pineapple juice
1 cup orange juice
1/4 cup butter
1 egg (slightly beaten)
1 tsp. salt
1/4 tsp. cinnamon
3 tbsp. brown sugar
1/3 cup cream

Peel the yams and cut into large chunks. Place these in a saucepan and add the fruit juices. Cook for 20 minutes or until the yams become tender. Then mash the yams. Next add the butter, egg, salt, cinnamon, brown sugar, and cream. Beat until the mixture is creamy, adding additional cream or juice if needed. Spoon this into a well-greased baking dish.

Topping:
1/4 cup sifted flour

3 tbsp. brown sugar
1/2 tsp. cinnamon
1/4 tsp. salt
3 tbsp. butter
1/4 cup chopped nuts
1 cup miniature marshmallows

Combine the flour with the brown sugar, cinnamon, and salt. Cut in the butter into this mixture and mix until it resembles small crumbs. Stir in the nuts, and then sprinkle the mixture over the yam mixture. Press the marshmallows, lightly, on top. Bake at 350 degrees for 25 minutes.

This recipe makes about 6 servings.

Spanish Rice

1 cup rice
1 lb. ground beef
1 green bell pepper
2 cups tomatoes
1/2 medium onion
3 tbsp. butter

Melt the butter, and then add the rice, beef, pepper, and onion. Then add the tomatoes. Let it simmer for 30 to 45 minutes.

Baked Beans

2 (15 oz.) cans pork and beans
Grated cheese (about 1/2 cup)
5 slices bacon (cut in small pieces)
1 small onion

1 small green pepper (if desired)
1 cup barbecue sauce
1/2 cup water

Mix all the ingredients together, and put into a 2-quart casserole dish and bake in oven at 350 degrees for 35 minutes or until onions are done.

Hash Browns

Mix the following ingredients together:
1/2 stick melted margarine
2 cans cream of celery soup
8 oz. sour cream
2 cups sharp cheese (grated)
1 small onion (grated or chopped)

Pour this mixture over a large box of hash browns, cover the top with corn flakes, and bake at 350 degrees for 1 hour.

Perfect Potato Salad

Sprinkle 5 cups cubed cooked potatoes with the following:
1 tsp. salt
2 tsp. sugar
1 tsp. celery seed
2 tsp. vinegar
And then add:
1/2 cup chopped onion
1 cup chopped celery
1/2 cup chopped sweet pickles
1 1/2 cup mayonnaise

Toss to mix, and fold in 4 sliced hard-boiled eggs, and then keep chilled until ready to serve.

Five Bean Casserole

1 lb. pork sausage
1/2 cup celery (diced)
1 onion (chopped)
1 can green beans (drained)
1 can yellow beans (drained)
1 can kidney beans (drained)
2 – 16 oz. cans pork and beans
1 can of tomato soup
1 cup dark brown sugar

Brown the sausage, celery, and the onion together. Pour off the fat. Add the other ingredients, and mix together thoroughly. Bake for 1 hour at 350 degrees. Bacon may be substituted, if desired.

Chicken Salad

2 chicken breasts (diced)
3/4 cup diced celery
11 oz. can mandarin oranges
1 cup green grapes
15 1/2 oz. can pineapple tidbits
Mix all the ingredients together thoroughly, and chill. Then top with the following dressing recipe.

Dressing: Mix 1/2 cup mayonnaise, 1/2 cup sour cream, 1 tsp. lemon juice, salt to taste, 1 tsp. herb dressing mix, and 1 tablespoon minced onion thoroughly.

Southern Slaw

4 cups fresh chopped cabbage
1/2 cup sugar
1/3 cup vinegar
1/2 cup cream

Dissolve sugar in the vinegar, stir in the cream, and beat until thick and creamy. Add just enough to the cabbage just to moisten before serving.

Luncheon Corn

Cook 1 cup broken macaroni in salted boiling water. Drain and rinse in cold water. Place in baking dish. Beat 1 egg; add 1 cup corn, 1 cup milk, 2 tsp. sugar, 1 tsp. salt. Pour over macaroni, and dot with butter. Bake at 325-350 degrees for about 20 minutes. Garnish with parsley or water cress. Cheese may be grated over the dish before baking for added flavor.

Baked Tomatoes

Wash tomatoes and cut into halves. Place on broiler with the cut side up. Sprinkle with bits of butter, grated cheese, salt, and pepper (to taste). Broil or bake until tender.

Southern Gumbo

Cut up 2 young chickens and fry in skillet; when brown put in a pot with 1 quart of finely chopped okra, 4 large tomatoes, and 2 chopped onions. Salt and pepper to your taste. Cover with boiling water. Let simmer and cover for 3 hours. Serve with boiled rice.

Main Dishes and Casseroles

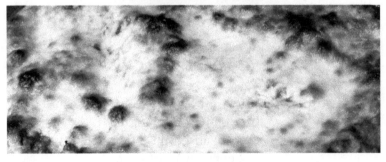

Italian Meatballs

1 lb. ground beef
1 egg
1/4 cup grated yellow onion
1/4 cup chopped green and red peppers
1/4 cup milk
1/2 cup bread crumbs
1 tablespoon Italian seasoning
2 cloves garlic, minced
Salt & pepper to taste
1/4 teaspoon red chili flakes
2 tbsp. chopped parsley
1/2 cup grated Parmesan cheese

Mix all ingredients together. Shape into meatballs about 2" diameter.

Brown in pan on medium heat. Finish cooking in a 350-degree oven for approximately 30 minutes.

Baked Macaroni and Cheese

1 1/2 cups dry elbow macaroni shells
3 tbsp. butter or margarine
3 tbsp. all-purpose flour
2 cups milk not skim
1/2 tsp. each salt and pepper
2 cups shredded cheese (can be sharp cheddar and mozzarella)

Preheat oven to 350 degrees.

Bring a pot of water to a boil; add salt to the pasta.

While the pasta cooks, melt butter in a skillet or pot large enough to hold the pasta when it's done.

Add the flour and stir over medium heat until lightly browned; 1-2 minutes.

Add the milk and whisk to remove any lumps and add the salt and pepper.

Cook over medium-high heat until the sauce thickens and starts to bubble. About 7 minutes.

Stir in the cheese and whisk until smooth and melted. Remove from heat.

When the pasta is almost done but still firm, drain it and add to the sauce.

Stir the pasta into the sauce and bake in a greased 2-quart dish for 20-25 minutes until browned and bubbly.

Sloppy Joes From Scratch

1 lb. ground beef
1/4 cup chopped onion
1/2 cup chili sauce
1/4 cup water
1 tbsp. cup prepared mustard
1 teaspoons chili powder
6 hamburger buns, split
cheddar cheese (shredded for topping)

In a large skillet, cook beef and onion until beef is browned, then drain. Add chili sauce, water, mustard and chili powder. Simmer, uncovered, for 20 minutes, stirring occasionally. Spoon onto each bun; top with cheddar cheese.

Stuffed Shells
Three Cheese Stuffed Shells Recipe

1 – 12 oz. Box - Jumbo Shells
4 Cups - Cottage Cheese
2 Cups - Mozzarella Cheese
1/2 Cup - Parmesan Cheese
2 Eggs
1 tbsp. - Dried Parsley
1 tsp. - Dried Oregano
1 tsp. - Salt
1 tsp. - Black Pepper
24 oz. - Spaghetti Sauce

Boil shells in salted water for 7 minutes (these will not be fully cooked)

Combine cottage cheese, mozzarella, Parmesan, eggs, parsley, oregano, salt and pepper until thoroughly mixed.

Drain shells and stuff with cheese mixture.

In a 9x13 baking dish add one cup of sauce, then one single layer of the stuffed shells.

Pour remaining sauce over the shells, cover with aluminum foil and bake at 350° for 30 minutes.

Uncover and top with 1/4 cup mozzarella cheese and place back in the oven uncovered for 10 minutes.

Let cool 10 minutes before serving.

Leftover Turkey Cornbread Casserole Recipe

2 tbsp. unsalted butter
1/2 cup diced yellow onion
1/2 cup diced carrots
1/2 cup diced celery
1/2 tsp. dried rosemary
1/2 tsp. dried thyme
1/2 tsp. dried nutmeg
1/2 tsp. dried ground sage
1/2 tsp. salt
1/4 tsp. pepper
1 lb. Turkey Breast (leftovers or from cooked breast)
cubed, (about 4 cups diced)
1 cup turkey gravy
1 (8.5 oz) corn muffin mix prepared according package
directions
1 (15 oz) can corn drained
1 (8 oz) block cheddar cheese shredded

Preheat oven to 400 degrees and grease a small rectangle
baking dish with cooking spray.

Melt butter in a medium sauté pan over medium heat.

Once melted, add in onion, carrots, celery, and spices.

Cook until vegetables are tender, about 10 minutes.

Once cooked, stir in cubed turkey and pour
vegetable/turkey mixture into the bottom of the prepared
baking dish.

Pour gravy over and set aside.
In a large bowl, mix together corn muffin mix according to
package directions.

Then stir in corn and cheddar cheese.

Pour corn muffin mixture over the vegetables/turkey.

Bake in preheated oven for 45-55 minutes, or until toothpick inserted comes out clean.

Cabbage Rolls

1 cup tomatoes (cooked)
1/2 cup cooked rice
1/2 cup milk
1/2 cup water
1 large head of cabbage
1 lb. ground beef
2 tsp. salt
1/2 tsp. pepper
2 tbsp. brown sugar

Cook rice. Remove leaves from cabbage and immerse them in hot water. Wipe them dry. Mix the meat, milk, add seasonings, and rice. Make small rolls of meat mixture, put in cabbage leaves and roll. Secure with toothpick. Pack cabbage rolls in pot and cover with large can of tomatoes. Cook covered over low heat for about 2 hours.

Homemade Pizza

2 1/2 to 3 cups all-purpose flour
1 tbsp. sugar
1 (1/4 oz.) package yeast
1 1/2 tsp. salt
1 cup very warm water (110 to 120 degrees)
2 tsp. oil

Combine 1 cup of flour, the sugar, yeast, and salt in a large bowl and blend thoroughly. Gradually add warm water and 2 tbsp. oil to the flour mixture. Blend at a low speed until moistened; beat for 2 minutes at medium speed, scraping bowl occasionally. By hand, stir in the additional 1 to 1 1/2 cups flour until dough pulls cleanly away from the sides of the bowl.

On a floured surface, knead in 1/4 to 1/2 cup flour until the dough is smooth and elastic, about 8 to 10 minutes. Cover loosely with plastic wrap, and let rest in a warm place for about 30 minutes.

Heat the oven to 450 degrees. Roll the dough into a 12" circle; place on lightly greased 12" pizza pan or large cookie sheet. Pinch the edge of the dough to create a rim. Prick the dough randomly with a fork. Let rest for 10 minutes. Pre-bake the crust at 450 degrees for 5 minutes. Remove crust from the oven and place on a wire rack.

You can then spread any generic pizza sauce from your local grocery store on top. Then top with 2 cups of mozzarella cheese (grated) and pepperoni or other desired meat. Then place back in the oven and cook until the cheese has melted evenly, about 6 minutes. Then remove from the oven let cool a little, slice, and serve.

Swedish Meatballs

1 1/2 lbs. ground meat
1 slice bread
1 egg
1/4 tsp. chili powder
1 1/2 tsp. oregano

1 to 2 tsp. ketchup
Salt and pepper to taste
Margarine for frying
Package of gravy mix

Put the meat in a bowl; wet the bread, squeeze out excess moisture and add the meat with the egg and seasonings. Mix thoroughly. Make them into small, round meatballs about one inch in diameter. Brown them in the margarine.

After the meatballs have been browned; drain off the excess fat, and add the package of gravy mix according to the directions on the package. Simmer in the pan for about 30 minutes, and serve hot with rice.

Lasagna

1 lb. Italian sausage (pork or beef)
1 clove of garlic (minced)
1 tablespoon chopped parsley
1 tablespoon basil
1 1/2 tsp. salt
1 (1lb.) can (2 cups) tomatoes
2 (6oz.) cans (1 1/2 cups) tomato paste
1 (10oz.) package lasagna noodles
2 (12oz.) cartons (3 cups) large curd cream style cottage cheese
2 beaten eggs
1/2 tsp. pepper
2 tbsp. chopped parsley
1/2 cup grated Parmesan cheese
1 lb. Mozzarella cheese (sliced thin)
Brown the meat slowly; spoon off excess fat. Add the next 6 ingredients to the meat. Simmer, uncovered, until thick, about 30 minutes, stirring occasionally.

Cook the noodles in boiling salted water until tender; drain; rinse in cold water.

Combine cottage cheese with next 5 ingredients. Place half of the noodles in a 13"x9"x2" baking dish; spread half of the cottage cheese mixture over them; add half of the Mozzarella cheese and half of the meat. Repeat layers.

Bake in moderate oven (375 degrees) for 30 minutes. Let stand 10 to 15 minutes before cutting into squares.

Leftover Turkey Casserole

1 cup turkey (shredded)
10 oz. can cream of mushroom soup
1 cup celery (chopped)
2 tsp. grated onions
3 oz. can chow mein noodles (set aside 1/2 cup)
1/2 cup water
1/2 cup nuts (sliced)

Mix all ingredients and place in greased baking dish. Top with remaining noodles. Bake at 325 degrees for 40 minutes.

"South of the Border" Casserole

1 green pepper (chopped)
1 large onion (chopped)
1 stick of margarine
1 can cream of mushroom soup
1 can cream of chicken soup
1 can beef broth

3 lbs. ground meat
1 package corn tortillas (12)
1 1/2 lb. cheddar cheese (grated)
1 can tomatoes (chopped)

Sauté the pepper and onion in the margarine. Add the soups and the broth to make sauce. Brown the meat, and season to taste and drain. In a 10x14 inch pan, layer 1/2 tortillas, 1/2 meat, 1/2 sauce, and 1/2 cheese. Add another layer. Put tomatoes on top and bake at 350 degrees for 45 minutes or until cheese is melted and bubbly on top.

Lasagna 2

1 box of lasagna noodles (about 9 noodles)
1 1/2 to 2 lbs. ground beef
1/3 cup onion (minced)
1 tsp. oregano
1/2 tsp. basil (optional)
1/4 tsp. garlic (minced)
1 tsp. salt (more if desired)
1/4 tsp. pepper
1/2 tsp. sugar (more if desired)
15/16 oz. can stewed tomatoes (drained and cut in pieces)
45 oz. can tomato sauce
2 eggs
1 lb. ricotta cheese
12 oz. mozzarella cheese (shredded)

Prepare noodles according to the directions on the box. Rinse under cool water and drain.
Crumble beef and onions in skillet and brown. Drain off the fat. Sprinkle the meat with oregano, basil, garlic, salt, pepper, and sugar. Add tomatoes and sauce, simmer at least 10 minutes. Taste, add more spices if needed.

Beat the eggs, add the ricotta cheese, and mix.

In 13"x9"x2" pan, cover bottom with sauce mixture.

Layer as follows: noodles, cheese mixture, sauce mixture, mozzarella cheese. Do this 3 times, and bake for 1 hour at 350 degrees.

Carrot-Celery Casserole

3 cups diagonally-sliced carrots
2 cups diagonally-sliced celery
1/4 cup melted butter
1 tsp. salt
1/8 tsp. pepper
1 tsp. sugar
1 tablespoon chopped parsley

Preheat oven to 350 degrees. Combine carrots and celery in greased 1 1/2-quart casserole dish. Mix in the rest of the ingredients. Bake (covered) for 45 minutes or until tender.

Meat, Poultry and Seafood

Hamburger Steaks with Mushroom & Onion Gravy

2 lbs. ground chuck or ground beef
32 oz beef broth
8 oz Portabella Mushrooms (sliced)
1 large yellow onion sliced
1/4 cup all-purpose flour
1 tbsp. Worcestershire Sauce
salt to taste
pepper to taste
garlic to taste

Form beef into 8 patties and season both sides with salt, pepper and garlic.

In a large skillet, brown patties over medium high heat for 4-5 minutes per side.

Remove the patties, add the onions and sauté for 5 minutes.

Add mushrooms and continue sauté another 2-3 minutes.

Add all-purpose flour, mix in until absorbed into the oil and cook 2-3 minutes to remove flour taste.

Add beef broth and Worcestershire, mix and simmer.

Add patties back in, spoon sauce over meat, cover, reduce the heat to low and let simmer for 1 hour.

Remove the lid, stir ingredients and let simmer another 5 minutes uncovered or until thickened.

Salisbury Steak Recipe

2 lbs. ground beef
1/2 Cup bread crumbs
1 egg
1/2 Cup Milk
1 tsp. salt
1 tsp. black pepper
2 tbsp. dried minced onion
1 tbsp. beef base
2 tbsp. Worcestershire sauce
2 medium yellow onions (chopped or sliced)
4 cups water
2 tbsp. corn starch mixed with 2 tbsp. water
2 cups sliced mushrooms (optional)

In a large bowl combine egg, milk, bread crumbs,
Worcestershire sauce, dried onions, black pepper, and salt.
Mix well.

Add ground beef and mix until well incorporated and form
into oval patties,

In a large skillet over medium heat, brown for 2 minutes
per side and remove from pan.

Add onions and mushrooms and sauté 2-3 minutes.

Add water and beef base, bring to a boil until the beef base
is dissolved.

Return patties to the skillet, return to a simmer, cover and
cook on low for 1 hour.

Add corn starch combination, mix until smooth and the
gravy has thickened.

BBQ Bacon Chicken Drumsticks

6 fresh chicken drumsticks/legs
6 bacon strips
1/2 cup barbecue sauce
1 tbsp. hot sauce
1 tbsp. honey
1 tsp. garlic powder
6 small sprigs fresh rosemary
1 tbsp. brown sugar

Preheat oven to 425°. Then, remove skin from each drumstick and discard.

In a medium bowl, combine barbecue sauce, hot sauce, honey, and garlic powder. Brush sauce all over chicken, then wrap each drumstick with a slice of bacon, tucking the ends under the bottom of the chicken. Sprinkle each drumstick with the brown sugar, then top with fresh rosemary.

Place chicken on a non-stick rimmed baking sheet and bake 35 to 40 minutes until the internal temperature of the chicken reaches 165° and bacon is crisp.

Chicken and Dumplings

Stew whole chicken. Then when tender pick the meat from the bones. Put the meat in a large pan with tight fitting lid and add 4 cups of broth. Bring to a boil.

Dumplings:
1 1/2 cups flour
3 tsp. baking powder
3/4 tsp. salt

1 1/2 tablespoon shortening
3/4 cup milk

Sift together the dry ingredients and cut in the shortening. Stir in enough milk, mixing only to moisten the dough thoroughly. Drop by the teaspoon into boiling chicken broth. Dip the spoon into the boiling liquid first so that the dough will slide off easily. Cover pan tightly and cook for 15 minutes. This makes enough for 6 servings.

Turkey Leftover

1 cup chopped turkey
1 tablespoon fat
2 tbsp. flour
1/2 tsp. salt
1 cup rolled corn flakes
1/8 tsp. pepper
1/2 tsp. chopped onion
2/3 cup bread crumbs
1 cup half cream, half milk
1 cup cream of chicken soup (diluted)

Melt fat in skillet, blend in flour, and add salt and pepper. Stir in milk. Cook on low heat stirring until thick. Stir in turkey, onion, and breadcrumbs. Shape into 8 small patties and chill. Dip in corn flakes, then in the milk and again into the corn flakes. Brown the patties in hot skillet and then place in bowl and cover with soup.

Goulash

1 large onion (chopped)
2 tbsp. butter
1 lb. ground beef
1 cup macaroni
1 cup tomato soup
3/4 cup water
salt and pepper to taste

Sauté the onions in the butter. Add ground beef and brown.
Season with salt and pepper to your taste. While onion and
meat are browning, cook the macaroni. When soft stir the
macaroni into the meat mixture, add tomato soup and
water. Simmer in heavy skillet, covered, for 15 minutes.
Serve with lettuce salad and corn bread.

Southern Fried Chicken

3 lb. chicken
1/2 cup milk (or evaporated)
1/2 cup water
2 tsp. salt
1/4 tsp. pepper
1 tsp. paprika
1 cup flour
1/2-inch cooking oil in a heavy skillet

Mix water and milk. Cut chicken and dip in liquid. Put dry
ingredients in paper bag. Heat oil to near smoking. Take
chicken from liquid, and put one at a time in paper bag and
shake. Take out of bag and put in skillet. Brown both sides
while covered tightly. Turn heat low and cook for 40
minutes. Uncover and turn heat up to crisp the chicken (5 to
10 minutes) turning once.

Hog Jowls and Turnip Greens (Southern Style)

Mustard, kale, and turnip greens are cooked same as spinach. Smoked hog jowl is then cooked with greens. Then season with red pepper and salt to taste. Cook until tender, drain and serve on platter with meat in center and poached eggs. It's usually served with cornbread.

Husband's Choice

Combine 1 lb. ground beef, 1/2 lb. ground lean pork, 1 cup bread crumbs (or crushed corn flakes), 1/2 cup sweet milk, 1 egg, 1 tablespoon brown sugar, and 1/4 tsp. cloves. Mix these together thoroughly.

Put mixture into 1 ½ quart greased ring mold and bake at 350 degrees for 45 minutes.

Baked Liver

For either beef or pork livers, cut into serving pieces, and dip 3 to 4 times in very hot water. Salt to taste and roll in flour. Melt 1/4 cup of shortening in a heavy skillet. Place liver in skillet, put onion slices on top of each piece of the meat. Bake at 315 degrees until tender and brown, then turn over.

Meat Loaf

1 lb. ground beef
1 egg (beaten)
1 cup corn flakes
1 cup tomato juice

1/2 lb. ground pork
1 cup bread crumbs (softened in 1 cup milk)
1 medium onion (chopped)
2 slices bacon
seasoning to taste

Mix the above ingredients. Form into a loaf. Place in pan, top with bacon slices, and pour extra cup of tomato juice over the top. Bake at 350 degrees for 1 to 1 ½ hours.

Corned Beef Hash Pie

1 lb. corned beef hash
1 egg (slightly beaten)
1/2 cup catsup
1 pint of peas or corn
1/4 lb. American cheese (grated)
3 tbsp. milk
1/8 tsp. dry mustard

Combine hash, egg, and catsup. Mix thoroughly. Line bottom and sides of greased 9" pie pan with this mixture. Spread the vegetables in top. Put cheese, milk, and mustard in saucepan. Heat until blended. Pour over meat-vegetable mixture. Bake at 350 degrees for 20 minutes. This makes 6 servings.

Applesauce Ham

Combine 1/4 cup applesauce, 1/3 cup honey, and 2 tbsp. prepared mustard and spread over a 1/2 inch ham slice.

Bake slowly for 1 hour 325-degree oven.

Baked Ham Glazes

Orange-Honey – Combine 1/2 cup with 1/2 cup orange juice and 1 cup light brown sugar. Mix thoroughly.

Currant Jelly – Blend together 1 cup currant jelly, 1/2 tsp. dry mustard, and 2 tbsp. prepared horseradish.

Cranberry – Fork whip 1 cup canned cranberry jelly with 1/2 cup light corn syrup.

Mustard – Combine 1 cup light brown sugar, 1/4 cup prepared yellow mustard, and 1/2 tsp. powdered cloves.

Ragout of Beef

For six pounds of the round, take half dozen ripe tomatoes, cut up with two or three onions in a vessel with a tight cover, add half a dozen cloves, a stick of cinnamon, and some fresh ground pepper. Cut gashes in the meat; stuff them with a half-pound of fat salt pork that has been cut into small bits. Place the meat on the other ingredients, and pour over it a half cup of vinegar and one cup of water; cover tightly and bake in a moderate oven; cook slowly four or five hours and, when about half done, salt to taste. When done, take out the meat, strain the gravy through a colander and thicken with flour.

Veal Loaf

Three and one-half pounds of lean and fat raw veal, chopped fine; one slice of salt pork, six crackers (rolled fine), butter the size of an egg, two eggs, one tablespoon of salt, one tablespoon of pepper, one of sage, three of extract of celery (or substitute one heaping tsp. of celery salt, eliminating the same amount of regular salt). Mix thoroughly. Pack tightly in a deep square tin; cover with bits of butter and sprinkle with cracker crumbs. Cover with another tin, and bake for two hours. Uncover and brown on top.

Chicken Tempura

2 broiler-fryers (2 to 3 lbs. each)
2 cups water
2 tsp. salt
1 tsp. poultry seasoning
1/4 tsp. pepper
2 eggs
1/2 cup milk
1 cup sifted flour
oil for frying

Cut each chicken into 8 pieces (2 breasts, 2 wings, 2 drumsticks, and 2 thighs); cook for 15 minutes in 2 cups water that is seasoned with 1 tsp. salt, poultry seasoning, and pepper. Drain the chicken on paper towels; remove all the skin and cut any small rib bones; dry thoroughly. Beat the eggs slightly with the milk in a bowl, and then beat in the flour and 1 tsp. salt until smooth. Add enough oil to make 2" depth in large heavy saucepan; heat to 375 degrees or use an electric fryer, following manufacturer's directions. Dip the chicken, one piece at a time, into batter (tongs are a useful tool); let any excess batter drip back into the bowl; fry 2 or 3 pieces at a time, turning once, about 4 minutes, or until golden; drain on paper towels; keep hot in warm oven while frying remaining chicken.

Virginia Crab Cakes

1 tablespoon butter
1/4 tsp. garlic (chopped)
1 tablespoon shallots (minced)
4 tbsp. bell pepper Brunoise
1 tsp. Old Bay seasoning
1 tsp. Dijon mustard
1 egg
1/2 cup mayonnaise
Juice of 1/2 lemon
1 lb. fresh crabmeat
1/8 cup bread crumbs
1/4 cup crackers (crumbled)
Salt and white pepper

Combine the butter, garlic, shallots, bell pepper, and Old Bay seasoning together in a small sauté pan and sweat over medium heat. In a mixing bowl, combine the Dijon mustard, egg, mayonnaise, and lemon juice with the cooked pepper mixture. Add the crab meat, bread crumbs, and crackers. Gently mix to combine, and season to taste with salt and pepper. Form into cakes and sauté to order.

Chicken Wings

1 lb. chicken wings
1/4 lb. butter (1 stick)
1/4 tsp. garlic powder
2 tbsp. parsley
1 cup fine, dry bread crumbs
1/2 cup Parmesan cheese
1 tsp. salt
1/4 tsp. pepper

Cut off the tips from the chicken wings and discard. Split the remaining portion of the wing at the joint to form two pieces.

Melt the butter and mix in the garlic powder. Combine with the bread crumbs, Parmesan cheese and seasonings. Dip the chicken wing portions in the seasoned butter, and then roll in the crumbs.

Bake on a greased baking sheet (use one with edges) in a preheated 325-degree oven for about 50 minutes.

Chicken Pot Pie

1 cup chopped onion
1 cup chopped celery
1 cup chopped carrot
1/3 cup melted butter or margarine
1/2 cup all-purpose flour
2 cups chicken broth
1 cup half and half
1 tsp. salt
1/4 tsp. pepper
4 cups chopped chicken
Parsley (optional)
Basic Pastry

Sauté the onion, celery, and carrot in butter for 10 minutes. Add flour to sautéed mixture, stirring well; cook 1 minute, stirring constantly. Combine the broth and half and half. Gradually stir in broth mixture; cook over medium heat, stirring constantly, until thickened and bubbly. Stir in the salt and pepper. Add the chicken, stirring well.

Pour the chicken mixture into a shallow 2-quart casserole. Top with pastry; cut slits to allow steam to escape. Bake it at 400 degrees for 40 minutes or until crust is golden brown. Garnish with parsley, if desired.

Basic Pastry:

1 cup all-purpose flour
1/2 tsp. salt
1/3 cup plus 1 tablespoon shortening
2 to 3 tbsp. cold water

Combine the flour and salt in a bowl; cut in the shortening with pastry blender until mixture resembles coarse meal. Sprinkle the cold water evenly over the surface; stir with fork until all dry ingredients are moistened. Shape into a ball and chill. Roll pastry for 9" pie.

Cabbage Rolls

1 small clove white garlic
1 small can sauerkraut
1 lb. ground chuck
1 egg
1 lb. pork
1 large cabbage head
1 small onion
1 large can tomato juice
Salt and pepper to taste

In a large pot, put ½ can of the kraut, a small amount of cabbage, and 2 cut up garlic pieces.

In another large bowl, put the meats, one egg, salt and pepper to taste, one onion (finely cut), and mix very well.

Then wrap the above into rolls. Put rolls in pot and cover with other ½ can kraut. Cover this with tomato juice and water, and cook for 1 ½ hours at medium heat.

Meat Loaf

1 lb. ground round beef
1 can tomatoes
1/2 cup finely chopped green pepper
1/2 cup chopped onion
6 to 8 single crackers
1/2 cup Minute rice (uncooked)
Salt and pepper

In a mixing bowl, crush the crackers. Then add the meat, peppers, onion, rice, salt, and pepper. Add about ¼ to ½ cup liquid from tomatoes. Break up tomatoes and put about ½ cup in the meat mixture. Mix thoroughly. Turn onto a greased baking dish (10"x10"). Place remaining tomatoes evenly on top of meat loaf. Add about the same amount of water to tomato liquid and pour around loaf. Add just a little more salt and pepper. Bake at 350 degrees for approximately 1 hour. Might take a little more time; the liquid will thicken and loaf will darken slightly around sides.

Quick Chicken 'N Dumplings

1 – 2 ½ to 3 lbs. frying chicken (cut into portion-sized pieces)
½ cup chopped onion (reserve 1 tablespoon for the dumplings)
2 thin slices lemon
1 small bay leaf
1 tsp. salt
¼ tsp. pepper
2 ½ cups warm water

Dumplings:
1 cup sifted flour
1 tsp. baking powder
½ tsp. salt
1 tablespoon chopped onion (reserved from above)
1/3 tsp. ground nutmeg
2 egg yolks (beaten)
½ cup half and half coffee cream

In a kettle with a tight-fitting cover, place the chicken, onion, lemon, bay leaf, salt, pepper, and warm water. Bring to a rolling boil and skim away any froth that gathers. Cover tightly and simmer for 30 minutes, or until the chicken breast can be pierced with a fork. Turn pieces of chicken over once or twice during this cooking period. Mix the flour, baking powder, salt, chopped onion, and nutmeg. Alternately add the beaten eggs and cream to the flour mixture, stirring after each addition. Mix until all is smoothly blended. Drop teaspoonfuls of this mixture on top of the bubbling chicken mixture. Close cover tightly again and cook at simmer for another 15 minutes without opening cover. When ready to serve, break dumplings apart with a fork, arrange on a platter with the chicken, and pour the remaining gravy over all.

Chinese Pepper Steak

1 lb. round steak (diced)
1/4 cup butter
1/4 cup onion (chopped)
1 tablespoon soy sauce
1/4 tsp. pepper
1 can beef consommé
1 can water
1/4 tsp. garlic salt
1 large green pepper
1/2 cup celery (chopped)
1 tablespoon cornstarch
1 tsp. water
3 cup rice (cooked)

Dice the steak and brown in butter. Add the onion, soy sauce, salt, pepper, consommé, water, garlic salt, green pepper, and celery. Cover and cook for 30 to 40 minutes.

Then add the cornstarch mixed with the 1 tsp. of water and cook 5 minutes longer. Serve over the rice.

Barbecued Spareribs

Spareribs
1/4 tsp. Tabasco sauce
1/8 tsp. chili powder
1 cup water
1 tablespoon brown sugar
1/2 cup ketchup
1 1/2 tsp. salt
1/2 tsp. mustard
Onions (sliced)

Place spareribs in bottom of heavy kettle. In medium saucepan combine the Tabasco sauce, chili powder, water, sugar, ketchup, salt, and mustard. Mix thoroughly. Cover spareribs with a layer of sliced onions, and then pour sauce over top. Repeat layers. Cover and bake at 325 degrees until meat is tender (about 2 to 2 ½ hours). Uncover last half hour and serve hot.

Schnitzel

1 1/2 lbs. sliced veal
Flour of coating
1 cup canned tomatoes
1/2 cup celery (diced)
2 T. bacon fat or cooking oil
3 tbsp. flour
1 small onion (chopped)
2 carrots (diced)

Coat the meat with flour and brown in melted fat. Remove meat from pan. To remaining fat, add 3 tbsp. flour and blend well. Add the tomatoes and stir until sauce begins to thicken. Add the meat and vegetables. Cover and simmer until meat is tender.

Chicken with Rice

1/2 cup margarine
1 cup regular rice
1 tsp. instant onion flakes
1 tsp. salt
10 1/2 oz. can mushroom soup
1 cup water
3 chicken breasts (cut in half or 1 whole chicken, cut up)

Coarse black pepper
4 oz. can of mushrooms (drained (optional)

Melt margarine in 9x13 inch baking dish. Stir in rice, onion flakes, salt, soup, and water. Place chicken over top of mixture and sprinkle with pepper. Bake at 350 degrees uncovered for 1 to 1 ¼ hours. You can add a 4 ounce can of drained mushrooms if you like.

Just Plain Meat Loaf

1 lb. hamburger
1 cup crushed cracker or bread crumbs
1 small onion (chopped fine)
1/2 tsp. salt
3 T. green pepper (chopped fine)
1 – 8 oz. can tomato sauce
2 tsp. chili powder (optional)

Mix all the ingredients and bake in a 6"x6" baking pan at 375 degrees for 50 minutes.

Chili

2 onions (finely chopped)
1 cup green pepper (finely chopped)
4 tbsp. vegetable oil
1 lb. ground chuck
1 clove of garlic (finely chopped)
1 package chili mix
4 tbsp. chili powder
Black pepper to taste
4 - 8 oz. cans tomato sauce.

Cook onion in oil until done. Cook the green pepper in oil until done. Brown the meat until done and stir in the onion, green pepper, garlic, chili mix, chili powder, and black pepper. Add the tomato sauce, and mix thoroughly. Add water and let simmer for 30 minutes, stirring often.

Mini Drum Sticks

24 broiler-fryer chicken wings
¾ cup potato chips (finely crushed)
½ cup wheat germ
¼ cup milk
1 egg

Cut chicken wings at the plumpest inner joint. Combine the wheat germ and crushed potato chips. Milk the milk and the egg. Dip the chicken in this mixture then in the wheat germ and chip mixture. Lie in a greased shallow baking pan and bat at 375 degrees for 45 minutes or until crispy brown and tender.

Scampi

2 lb. fresh shrimp (de-veined, peeled (except for tail shells))
3/4 cup butter
2 cloves garlic (minced)
Juice of 1 lemon
Salt and white pepper to taste
Chopped parsley to garnish

Melt butter in small skillet over moderate heat; add garlic and lemon juice. Simmer 3 minutes, stirring often. Place shrimp on tin foil broiler pan, pour garlic sauce over and sprinkle with salt and pepper. Place in preheated broiler 4 inches from heat; broil 5 to 7 minutes, turning each shrimp once when lightly browned. Serve shrimp with pan juices, topped with the parsley.

Basic Pot Roast

3 to 4 lb. beef pot roast
3 tbsp. fat
2 tsp. salt
1/4 tsp. pepper
1 medium onion (sliced)
1/2 cup water

Brown the meat thoroughly in the hot fat in a Dutch oven or other heavy utensil. Sprinkle with salt and pepper. Add the onion and water, cover pan tightly and simmer over low heat, 2 ½ to 3 hours or until very tender when pierced with a fork. (Pot roast, also, may be cooked in a covered roaster in a 325 degrees oven.)

To make gravy, skim off all but about 2 to 3 tbsp. of fat and add enough water so that amount in pan equals about 2 cups. Mix the 3 tbsp. of flour to a smooth paste with a few tbsp. of water and stir into liquid. Cook until thickened, stirring constantly. Season to taste with the salt and pepper.

(About an hour before end of cooking time, vegetables may be added, such as 6 medium carrots (scraped), 6 small potatoes (pared), and 6 medium onions (peeled).)

Pan Fried Chicken Schnitzel-Style

4 boneless chicken breasts (4oz each)
1 1/2 cups breadcrumbs, dry
1/2 cup all-purpose flour
2 eggs
3/4 cup milk
2 tablespoons dried herbs (thyme, basil, rosemary, and chives)
salt & ground black pepper, to taste
olive oil, for sautéing
1 fresh lemon, cut into 8 wedges

Whisk eggs and mix with milk.

Mix the chopped herbs with the bread crumbs.

Cut each chicken breast in half (widthwise to make them thin) and place between two pieces of plastic wrap and pound them evenly with a butcher's mallet until they are 1/8 of an inch thick.

Season with salt and fresh cracked black pepper.

Lightly coat each piece with all-purpose flour.
Dip each piece in the egg wash and then coat each piece with the herbed bread crumbs.

Heat a pan to medium heat and sauté the chicken in olive oil for 2 – 3 minutes per side.

Pot Roast

3 lbs. beef roast
2 tablespoons oil
1 cup chopped onion
4 cups beef broth
5 carrots, 1 in chunks
5 potatoes, 2 in chunks
1 1/2 cups sliced celery
1 teaspoon salt
1 teaspoon pepper
1 teaspoon oregano
1 bay leaf
1/2 teaspoon thyme
1 cup diced tomato

In Dutch oven, brown roast in oil.
Add onions and sauté briefly.
Add broth; cover and cook on low for 2 hours; add
more broth if necessary.

Add all other ingredients. Bring to a boil.

Reduce heat to low and cook for 1-1/2 hours more.

Beef and Pepper Skillet

1-pound lean ground beef
1 can diced tomatoes with mild green chiles, undrained
1 cup of water
14 oz. beef broth
1 tbsp chili powder
1/4 tsp salt
1/8 tsp garlic powder
1 tbsp beef bouillon

2 cups instant white or brown rice
1 cup green and red Peppers
1 cup shredded Colby-Monterey Jack cheese

In a large cast-iron or other heavy skillet, cook beef over medium heat until no longer pink,6-8 minutes, breaking into crumbles; drain.

Add tomatoes, broth, chili powder, salt and garlic powder; bring to a boil. Stir in rice and peppers. Reduce heat; simmer, covered, until liquid is absorbed, 8-10 minutes. Remove from heat; sprinkle with cheese. Let stand, covered, until cheese is melted.

Oven Barbecued Pork Chops

4 thick cut bone-in pork chop
salt and pepper
1 cup ketchup
1/2 cup chili sauce
1/4 cup packed light brown sugar
2 tablespoons honey
1 tablespoon Worcestershire sauce
1 tablespoon yellow mustard
1 teaspoon apple cider vinegar
1/2 teaspoon paprika
1/2 teaspoon garlic powder
1/4 teaspoon cayenne pepper
1/4 teaspoon celery salt, optional

Preheat oven to 350 degrees and grease a 9x13-inch baking dish. Season pork chops with salt and pepper and place in baking dish.

In a medium bowl, stir together remaining ingredients.

Pour over pork chops.

Cover with foil and bake 45 to 50 minutes.
Uncover, flip pork chops over and spoon sauce on top.
Bake another 10 minutes.

Spoon sauce over top again and broil 2 to 5 minutes, or
until sauce is bubbly and thickened.

Pork Chops with Onions and Bell Peppers

3 tbsp olive oil
2 or more pork chops thick cut
1 1/2 tbsp Adobo seasoning
1 tbsp Memphis Style BBQ seasoning
1 1/2 tsp steak seasoning
1 tsp chili powder
1 tsp paprika
1/2 tsp salt
1/4 tsp black pepper
3/4 or more cup Onion Pepper Blend

In a large frying pan add olive oil and heat before adding
pork chops.

When pan is heated, add pork chops and sprinkle with each
seasoning.

Cook until chops are almost done, then add Onion Pepper
Blend. Allow to cook until pork chops are done and the
peppers are cooked through.

Pies, Pastry and Dessert

Easy Pumpkin Pie Cheesecake Recipe

2 (8 oz) packages cream cheese at room temperature
1/2 cup granulated sugar
1 teaspoon vanilla extract
2 large eggs
1/2 cup pumpkin puree
2 teaspoons pumpkin spice
1 (9-inch) graham cracker crust (store bought or homemade)
Whipped Cream, optional

Preheat oven to 325°F.

In a large bowl, combine cream cheese, granulated sugar and vanilla extract. Beat until well combined. Blend in eggs one at a time, until smooth.

Remove 1 1/3 cups of the cheesecake batter and pour it into the bottom of the graham cracker crust; set aside.

Add the pumpkin puree and pumpkin spice to the remaining cheesecake batter and whisk gently until well combined. Carefully spread the pumpkin layer over the plain cheesecake layer with a spatula.

Bake in preheated oven for 35 to 40 minutes, or until center is almost set. Allow to cool (about 1 hour), then refrigerate for a minimum of 3 hours or overnight.

Serve with whipped cream (optional).

Tennessee Peach Pudding

1 cup all-purpose flour
1/2 cup granulated sugar
2 teaspoons baking powder
1/2 teaspoon salt
1/2 teaspoon ground cinnamon, optional
1/2 cup milk
3 cups sliced peeled peaches (fresh or frozen)

Topping:
1 1/2 cups water
1/2 cup granulated sugar
1/2 cup brown sugar, packed
1 tablespoon butter
1/4 teaspoon ground nutmeg
Vanilla ice cream (optional)

Preheat the oven to 400 degrees. Grease an 8-inch baking dish with oil or butter.

Mix the flour, sugar, baking powder, salt, and cinnamon, if using. Pour the milk and stir until combined. Using a spatula, carefully mix in the peaches.

Pour the batter into the baking dish.

For the topping, stir together the water, sugars, butter, and nutmeg in a large saucepan over medium heat. Bring the mixture to a boil, stirring constantly, until the sugars are dissolved. Pour the syrup over the peach batter.

Bake for 40 to 50 minutes, or until a toothpick inserted into the center comes out clean. Serve warm or cold with vanilla ice cream.

Grandma's Fried Apple Pies

1 can of apples or about 4 apples peeled cut and cooked
2 cups granulated sugar
4 heaping cups self-rising flour
3/4 cup shortening
1/4 cup unsalted butter
1 1/2 - 2 cups ice water

Additional flour for mixing dough
2 cups shortening
4 tablespoons butter

For apples:
Put apples in a large pot or Dutch oven and add enough water to almost cover. Stir in two cups sugar.

Turn heat to medium-high and bring to a boil.

Turn heat down just a little, so apples continue to simmer, breaking up apples with spoon as they cook. Cook until apples are tender and juicy, stirring frequently. You may need to add more water as they cook. Do not allow the apples to get dry. Remove apples from heat and allow to cool.

For dough:
Start with 4 heaping cups of self-rising flour and cut in 3/4 cup shortening and 1/4 cup butter with a fork or your fingers. Mix well until shortening/butter is incorporated into the flour.

Add 1 1/2 cups of ice water to flour, and add additional ice water as needed to get all the dry flour mixed in. Mix with a fork until dough is sticky.

Dip hands in flour and sprinkle additional flour onto dough so that you can knead it. Use additional flour as needed to be able to knead the dough until smooth and non-sticky. Pinch off pieces of dough to make balls slightly smaller than ping pong balls.

Roll each ball out until thin.

Add a heaping spoonful or two of apples to one side of rolled dough. After the first couple, you will learn exactly how much apples to place on the dough. If you put too much, the dough will not cover without tearing.

Dip your finger in water and rub around the edges of the dough where the apples are.

Carefully fold the dough over and press the edges together lightly to seal. Using a fork, crimp the edges to fully seal. Once all the pies are ready, add about ½ cup Crisco shortening and 2 tablespoons butter to a large skillet and heat on medium-high.

Once the oil is hot enough to sizzle from a drop of water, carefully lay two or three pies in the skillet.

Cook about a minute to a minute and half on each side until they are golden brown.

Lay pies on a large platter lined with paper towels and serve immediately.

Pickled Peaches

One pint cooked peach halves. To the syrup, add 3/4 cup firmly packed brown sugar, 1/2 cup vinegar, two 3" sticks of cinnamon, 1 tsp. whole cloves, 1 tsp. all spice. Boil 5 minutes. Add the peach halves and simmer for another 5 minutes. Chill in syrup several hours or overnight. They are quick and easy and delicious with meats or on a party plate.

Spiced Grapes

Wash a gallon of grapes and remove hulls from pulp. Heat the pulp 10 minutes. Then run through a sieve to remove the seeds. Put pulp and hulls in a pan. Add 4 lb. sugar, 2 tsp. of ground cinnamon, 2 tsp. of ground cloves, 1 pint vinegar. Cook (stirring often) until it is the consistency of preserves. Pour into small, sterile jars and seal. They are very good when served with meat.

Apple Relish

Grind 2 hot peppers and 5 onions. Add 1 tablespoon salt, and one cup boiling water. Let it stand 15 minutes and drain. Then add 14 large red apples that have been chopped with skins left on (cores removed), 1 quart vinegar, 1 cup sugar, and a cloth bag with tablespoon of whole spice, a tablespoon of cloves, and a stick of cinnamon inside. Cook for 10 to 15 minutes. Remove cloth bag and put in sterilized jars and seal.

Pumpkin Pie

2 eggs (slightly beaten)
3/4 cup sugar
1 tsp. cinnamon
1/2 tsp. ginger
1/4 tsp. cloves
1 3/4 cups pumpkin
1/2 tsp. salt
1 2/3 cup light cream
Unbaked pie shell

Mix in order listed, and pour into unbaked pie shell. Bake at 425 degrees for 15 minutes, then at 350 degrees for about 45 minutes or until inserted knife comes out clean. Let it cool and serve with whipped cream if desired.

Pecan Pie

Unbaked pie shell
1/2 cup butter
1/2 cup sugar
1/4 cup maple flavored syrup
3/4 cup white corn syrup
3 eggs (beaten)
1 tsp. vanilla
1 to 2 cups pecans

Preheat oven to 350 degrees. Cream butter and mix in sugar, syrups, eggs, and vanilla. Pour into pie shell. Arrange the pecans on top (you can chop the nuts and mix before pouring into shell if you like). Bake at 350 degrees for 1 hour.

Mock Apple Pie

Uncooked pie shell
2 cups water
2 tsp. cream of tartar
25 crackers
1 1/2 cups sugar

Bring water to a boil, and then drop in crackers. Place in the uncooked shell. Sprinkle with cinnamon and put dabs of butter on top. Bake this at 350 degrees for about 30 minutes.

Rhubarb Pie

Unbaked pie shell
2 cups cooked and cooled rhubarb
2 egg yolks
1 tablespoon corn starch
1/2 cup milk
1 cup sugar

Mix ingredients and stir thoroughly. Put these into the unbaked shell, dot top with butter and bake until firm. Top with egg whites beaten stiff with ¼ cup sugar. Return to oven until it's a golden brown. Bake at 350 degrees.

Lemon Icebox Pie

Beat 3 egg yolks slightly in top of double boiler, add ½ cup sugar and stir well. Add ½ tsp. salt, ¼ cup lemon juice to the above mixture and cook in double boiler to a custard-like consistency. Let cool. Add ½ cup chilled whipped cream to lemon mixture. Fold in 3 beaten egg whites.

Prepare 3 to 4 cups vanilla cookie crumbs; sprinkle half of crumbs on bottom of an ice tray. Put in the pudding, sprinkle other half of crumbs on top of pudding and freeze.

Buttermilk Pie

Cream 1 1/2 cups brown sugar, 1 1/2 cups white sugar, and 1 stick butter. Add 2 tbsp. of flour, 6 eggs (one at a time), 1/2 cup buttermilk, 1 1/4 tsp. of vanilla, and 1/2 tsp. salt. Pour into unbaked pie shell. Bake at 350 degrees for about 30 minutes. Do not over bake as this tends to make the pie watery. This will make 2 pies.

Apple Pie

1 unbaked 9" pie shell
3 or 4 large tart baking apples (About 2 lbs.)
1/2 cup sugar (for filling)
2 tbsp. flour (for filling)
1/2 tsp. nutmeg (for filling)
2 T. lemon juice (for topping)
1/2 cup sugar
1/2 cup flour
1/2 cup (1 stick) butter

Pare and slice apples in large bowl. Mix the ingredients for filling and sprinkle over slices. Drizzle with lemon juice. Toss to cover completely with the juice. Place in pie shell. Combine 1/2 cup sugar and 1/2 cup flour for topping in small bowl. Cut up the butter, sprinkle over the apples. Slide the pie into a heavy brown paper bag, large enough to cover pie loosely. Fold open end over twice and fasten with paper clips. Place on large cookie sheet. Bake at 425 degrees for 1 hour.

Southern Peanut Butter Pie

1 pie crust
3 eggs
1 cup dark corn syrup
1/2 cup granulated sugar
1/2 cup creamy-style peanut butter
1/2 tsp. vanilla
1 cup salted peanuts

Have the pie crust chilled when you start. Beat the eggs then add the corn syrup, sugar, peanut butter, and vanilla. Beat until smooth and then stir in the peanuts. Pour filling into the chilled shell and bake for 15 minutes in 400 degrees preheated oven. Then turn the heat down to 350 degrees and bake for 30 to 35 minutes. Serving after let to cool is best.

Green Tomato Pie

3 cups of sliced green tomatoes
1 1/2 cup sugar
1/4 tsp. salt
5 tsp. grated lemon rind
1/4 tsp. cinnamon
5 tbsp. butter
1 unbaked pie shell

Arrange the tomatoes in layers in the pie shell. Mix the other ingredients together in a bowl and sprinkle each layer of tomatoes with this mixture. When the bottom crust is filled, cover with a top crust, and bake at 350 degrees for 35 to 40 minutes.

Squash Pie

1 pint boiled dry squash
1 cup brown sugar
3 eggs
2 tsp. molasses
1 tsp. butter
1 tsp. ginger
1 tsp. cinnamon
1/2 tsp. salt
1 pint milk

Beat eggs and add remaining ingredients. Bake as a custard pie (in an unbaked pie shell) in a 350-degree oven.

Old Fashioned Custard Pie

Heat 1 quart of sweet milk almost to a boil, beat in 2 cups sugar, 8 eggs, and 2 tbsp. cornstarch. Place mixture in unbaked pie shell. Bake for 30 to 40 minutes in 300-degree oven.

Vinegar Pie

1 egg
3 tbsp. cider vinegar
1 tsp. lemon extract
4 tbsp. flour
1 cup sugar
1 cup boiling water
1 baked pie shell

Mix sugar and flour together, add boiling water, cook this for 5 minutes. Add beaten egg, cook 2 minutes. Add lemon and vinegar. Put in pie shell. Cool. Yolk can be used in pie and the white for meringue.

Never Fail Pastry

1 cup flour
1/4 tsp. baking powder
1/4 tsp. salt
4 tbsp. ice water
3 tbsp. shortening

Mix dry ingredients, cut in shortening and then add water to make very stiff dough. This will be enough for 1 pie shell.

Pastry

3/4 cup vegetable shortening
1/4 cup boiling water
1 tablespoon
2 cups sifted flour
1 tsp. salt

Put shortening in medium bowl. Add water and milk. Break up shortening with 4-prong fork. Tilt bowl and beat with fork in quick, cross-the-bowl strokes until mixture is smooth and thick like whipped cream and holds soft peaks when fork is lifted. Sift flour and salt onto shortening. With vigorous, round-the-bowl strokes, stir quickly, forming dough that clings together and cleans the bowl. Pick up dough and work into a smooth, flat round, then divide in half and form into balls. Roll out and cut out for one 2-crust pie.

Sweet Potato Pie

(Makes filling for a 9" crust.)
1/4 tsp. nutmeg
1 tsp. baking powder
1/2 cup milk
1/2 tsp. grated orange rind
1 tsp. brandy extract
3 medium-sized sweet potatoes
1/4 cup butter (at room temperature)
2 eggs (separated)
1/2 cup strained honey
1/4 tsp. salt

Place rack 4 to 5 inches from bottom of oven. Preheat oven to 450 degrees.

Make pastry. Roll out and line 9" pie pan, filling well into angels. Trim off with scissors, 1/2" beyond pan rim; turn overhang under so fold is even with pan rim. Crimp edge with fork or flute with fingers.

Cover pastry-lined pan with wax paper. Scrub potatoes in cold water, place in 3-quart saucepan, and cover with boiling water.

Heat to a boil, and reduce to a gentle boil. Cover pan, cook potatoes until soft. Drain potatoes, skin while hot and rub them through food mill or sieve to remove fibers.

Cool slightly. Beat in butter, egg yolks, and the rest of the unused ingredients until smooth and creamy.

Pour mixture into pan. Bake at 450 degrees for 15 minutes.

Reduce the heat to 300 degrees and bake for 25 to 30 minutes.

Lift pie from oven, spread with meringue (2 beaten egg whites, 3 tbsp. sugar). Be sure meringue touches crust all around and is smooth or swirled over top.

Return to oven for 20 minutes to brown meringue. Remove and cool 2 to 3 hours before cutting. This can serve 5 to 6.

Sweet Potato Pudding

Boil and smash 6 medium sweet potatoes. Add 2 whole beaten eggs, 1/4 lb. butter, 3/4 cup brown sugar, 1/2 cup milk, 2/3 cup flour, 1/4 cup orange juice, and 1 tsp. vanilla.

Put in buttered-greased shallow baking dish. Place thin slices of orange on top, and then bake for 30 minutes at 350 degrees or until slightly brown at the edges.

Peach Dumplings

3 cups sliced fresh peaches
2 cups water
1 cup sugar
2 tbsp. lemon juice
1 cup pancake mix
1/4 cup firmly packed brown sugar
1/4 tsp. nutmeg
1/2 cup milk
2 tablespoon melted oleo

Combine the peaches, water, sugar, and lemon juice in a 3-quart saucepan, and bring to a boil. Combine the remaining ingredients, stirring lightly. Drop the batter from tablespoon on hot peach mixture. Reduce the heat; cover tightly; cook for 15 minutes <u>without lifting the cover</u>. This is important! Serve warm with plain cream or peach or vanilla ice cream.

Maple Apples

5 medium sweet potatoes
5 medium tart apples
1 cup maple syrup
1/4 cup butter
Buttered crumbs

Boil sweet potatoes in their skins in salted water. While potatoes are boiling, pare and slice the apples and place in maple syrup. Add butter and a pinch of salt, cook until apples are tender. Peel potatoes and slice in halves, place in buttered baking dish. Spoon this over half of the apple syrup mixture. Repeat in layers. Top generously with buttered crumbs. Bake at 400 degrees long enough for the dish to be heated through and to brown crumbs.

Fried Apple Rings

Cut tart apples in rings about 1/2" wide. Remove core. Sprinkle both sides of apple slices with 2 tbsp. sugar. Cook in 1/8" hot fat on low heat until tender and glazed, about 5 minutes. A heavier skillet may take longer.

Sweet Potato Pie

2 cups sugar
3 eggs
1 tsp. nutmeg

2 T. vanilla
1 stick margarine or butter
2 cups cooked mashed sweet potatoes
1 cup milk
2 unbaked (9") pie shells

Mix all the ingredients in a large bowl. Pour this into the pie shells and bake in a preheated oven at 350 degrees until inserted knife comes out clean, about 40 to 45 minutes.

Blackberry Pan Pie

1 stick margarine
1/2 cup sugar
Blackberries (about 1 cup)
1 cup flour
1 tsp. salt
3 tsp. baking powder

Melt the margarine and sugar in a pan. Add the blackberries. Mix the flour, milk, sugar, salt, and baking powder and mix and pour over the blackberries. Cook at 350 degrees until the batter is set.

Peach Pie

Pastry for 2-crust 9" pie
6 cups peeled and sliced peaches
1/2 cup sugar
3 tbsp. cornstarch
Dash salt
1/2 tsp. ground nutmeg
1/2 cup sour cream
Milk

Sugar

Roll out half of the pastry. Use to line the bottom of a 9"
pie plate. Place the peaches in the pastry-lined pie plate.
In a small bowl, mix the sugar, corn starch, salt, nutmeg,
and sour cream. Pour this over the peaches. Roll out the
remaining pastry and make a lattice top. Brush the pastry
with milk and sprinkle with sugar. Bake at 425 degrees for
10 minutes. Reduce the heat to 350 degrees, and continue
baking for 45 to 50 minutes longer. Let cool on a rack
before serving. The recipe can serve 6 to 8.

Hershey Bar Pie

1/2 cup milk
1 (4oz.) Hershey bar with almonds
18 large marshmallows
1/2-pint heavy whipping cream
1 graham cracker crust

In top of a double boiler melt the Hershey bar along with
the milk and marshmallows. Whip the cream in a bowl
until it becomes stiff and fold this into the chocolate
mixture. Pour the mixture into the crust and place in the
refrigerator to cool. When it's cool, place it in the freezer.
Remove at dinner time and the pie will be thawed for
dessert. It will keep indefinitely (if covered properly) in
freezer.

Momma G's Cobbler Pie

1 stick margarine
1 cup sugar
3/4 cup milk

2 1/2 tsp. baking powder
Fruit

Melt the margarine in a pan. Mix the sugar, flour, milk, and the baking powder together thoroughly. Pour over the margarine, mix. Pour the fruit into the batter. Bake at 350 degrees for 40 minutes.

Country Cobbler

1 cup sugar
2 tbsp. tapioca
1/4 tsp. cinnamon
1/4 cup water
1/2 cup walnuts (chopped) or raisins
6 cups apple slices (thinly sliced and peeled)
1 cup flour
1/3 cup sugar
1 1/2 tsp. baking powder
1/2 tsp. salt
1 1/2 cups shredded sharp cheddar cheese
1/2 cup margarine (melted)
1/4 cup milk

Combine the sugar together with the tapioca, cinnamon, and water in a saucepan. Add the walnuts or raisins. Cook, stirring constantly, until mixture boils. Remove from the heat, and stir in the apples. Pour over 8" square baking dish. Sift together the dry ingredients. Stir in the cheese. Add the margarine and milk. Mix until just moistened. Spoon this over the apple mixture. Bake at 275 degrees for 35 to 40 minutes or until golden brown. Serve with whipped topping, if desired.

Rice Pudding

In a bowl combine 2 well beaten eggs, 1/3 – 1/2 cup sugar, and 1/4 tsp. salt. To this gradually add 2 cups of scalded milk and stir to blend thoroughly. Add 1 1/4 cups of cooked and cooled rice, 1 cup of raisins, 1 tsp. vanilla, a dash of cinnamon, and a dash of nutmeg. Pour this into a greased 1 1/2-quart casserole dish. Sit in a shallow pan partially filled with water. Bake in moderate oven (325 degrees) for about 1 hour.

Mother's Pecan Pie

3 eggs (slightly beaten)
1 cup dark corn syrup
1 cup sugar
2 tbsp. melted margarine
1 tsp. vanilla extract
Pinch of salt
1 cup pecans
1 unbaked 9" pie shell

Combine the first 6 ingredients in a bowl, and mix thoroughly. Stir in the pecans, pour into the pie shell, and bake at 400 degrees for 15 minutes. Reduce the temperature to 350 degrees and bake for another 30 to 35 minutes or until it becomes firm around the edges.

Custard
Whipped Cream

Mix the first five ingredients thoroughly. Then pour into layer cake pans. Bake in a 375-degree preheated oven for 20 minutes or until golden brown. Let cool. Next split the layers through the centers crosswise. Spread the Custard (recipe below) between the layers; cover the cake with the whipped cream.

Custard: Bring 2 cups of milk to the boiling point. Separately mix 1 cup sugar with 1/2 cup flour and 2 eggs. Then you can stir this into the milk. Add 1 tablespoon butter, stir until the mixture thickens, and then stir in a little vanilla. Let cool and use in the above recipe.

Homemade Pumpkin Pie

3/4 cup sugar
1/2 tsp. salt
1 3/4 tsp. pumpkin pie spice
1 can (15 oz.) Pure Pumpkin
2 large eggs (beaten)
1 can evaporated milk
1 carton whipped cream

Mix the sugar, salt, and spice in a small bowl. Next stir the pumpkin and eggs together then add this to the sugar mixture. Gradually stir in the evaporated milk. Then pour this into a pie shell. Bake this in a 425-degree preheated oven for 15 minutes. Reduce the temperature 350 degrees and bake for another 40 to 50 minutes or until a knife inserted near the center comes out clean. Let cool on a wire rack for 2 hours. You can either serve immediately or refrigerate. Top with whipped cream before serving. This recipe makes about 8 servings.

Heavenly Hash

1 (15 1/4 oz.) can crushed pineapple
1 can mandarin oranges
4 oz. cream cheese
1 medium container Cool Whip
1 small package coconut
1/2 bag miniature marshmallows

Drain the pineapple, and mandarin oranges. Mix the pineapple, oranges, coconut, and marshmallows together. In another bowl, blend the Cool Whip and softened cream cheese together. Then mix all ingredients together and chill.

Chocolate Pie

1 cup sugar
3 tbsp. cocoa
4 tbsp. flour
2 cups milk
1 tsp. vanilla
1 tsp. butter
2 egg yolks

Mix the cocoa, sugar, and flour together thoroughly. Beat in the egg yolks, and then add the milk, vanilla, and butter. Cook in a double boiler until thick.

Mama's From Scratch Chocolate Pudding Pie

For the **chocolate filling**
1 deep dish pie crust
1/4 cup cocoa
1/4 cup all-purpose flour

1/3 cup sugar
3 egg yolks, beaten
1 and 1/2 cup whole milk
1 teaspoon vanilla extract
2 tablespoon real butter

For the **meringue**
3 egg whites
1/4 cup granulated sugar
1 teaspoon vanilla extract

Prepare pie crust as directed on package for 1 9-inch pie crust. Cool 10 minutes.

For the **chocolate filling**

In a large saucepan at medium temperature, stir together sugar and egg yolks.

Stir in flour and cocoa powder. Add milk and stir gently to combine.

Stir continually on medium-low heat until pudding becomes thick.

Take off heat and stir in butter and vanilla. Stir until butter melts.

Pour into pie crust. Top with meringue or whipped cream.

For the **meringue**

Preheat oven to 350 degrees.

Place egg whites in the bowl of an electric mixer. Beat until soft peaks begin to form.

Slowly add sugar. Beat until they form stiff, glossy peaks.

Fold in vanilla

Spread meringue over pie.

Bake for 8 to 10 minutes or until golden brown

Coconut Custard Pie

1 1/2 cups milk
1 1/2 tbsp. flour
3 eggs
1/4 lb. dry coconut
1 1/2 cups sugar
1 tsp. vanilla
1 unbaked pie shell

Beat the eggs and sugar until creamy. Mix the coconut and flour together, and then add this to the eggs and sugar. Add the milk and vanilla and stir until well blended.

Pour into the unbaked pie shell and bake at 350 degrees for about 45 minutes.

Crunchy Ice-Cream Squares

2 cups coarsely crushed corn flakes
1 can (3 1/2 oz.) flaked coconut (1 1/2 cups)
1/2 cups chopped nuts
1/2 cup brown sugar
1/2 cup butter or margarine (melted)
1/2 gallon of favorite ice-cream

Mix the cereal, coconut, nuts, sugar, and butter. Press at least 2/3 of the cereal mixture evenly into an un-greased 13"x9"x2" pan. Pack the ice cream over the cereal layer; press to make even. Sprinkle remaining of the cereal mixture on top. Freeze until firm, at least 12 hours. Can make up to 15 servings

Watergate Salad

8 oz. container whipped cream
1 small package pistachio-flavored pudding
2 – 8 oz. cans of crushed pineapple (not drained)
1 cup miniature marshmallows
1/3 cup pecans (finely chopped)
Combine all ingredients thoroughly and refrigerate overnight.

Quiche

1 can crab, tuna or 1 cup ham, cut up
1 1/2 cup Munster or Swiss cheese
1/2 cup green pepper (chopped)
1/2 cup green onions (minced)
4 oz. can of mushrooms
2 large eggs

1/2 cup mayonnaise
1/2 cup milk
1/4 tsp. garlic salt
1 1/2 tablespoon cornstarch

In a large bowl toss the fish or meat with the cheese, peppers, onions, and mushrooms. Spoon into baked 9" deep ready-made pie shell or make your own. In a small bowl, beat together eggs, mayonnaise, milk, garlic salt, and cornstarch. Pour over cheese mixture. Cover the edge of the shell with foil so it doesn't burn. Bake at 350 minutes for 55 minutes or until knife comes out clean. Let cool for 5 minutes before cutting.

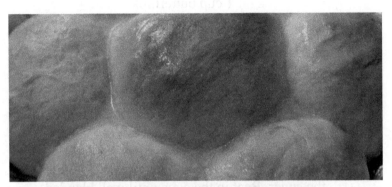

Breads and Rolls

Easy Buttermilk Cornbread Muffins

1/2 cup salted butter melted
2/3 cup granulated sugar
2 large eggs
1 cup buttermilk
1/2 tsp. baking soda
1 cup cornmeal
1 cup all-purpose flour
1/2 teaspoon table salt

Preheat the oven to 375 degrees. Grease a muffin tin or line it with cupcake liners.

In a medium-sized bowl combine the melted butter with the sugar. Beat in the eggs until well blended.

Add in the baking soda and then slowly pour in the buttermilk while you stir.

Add in the cornmeal, flour, and salt and stir until well combined. Pour batter into the prepared muffin tin.

Bake in the 375-degree oven for about 20 minutes, until the tops start to brown.

No Knead Yeast Dinner Rolls

2 packets rapid rise yeast
1/4 cup sugar
1 tsp. sugar (for yeast to feed off of)
1 1/3 cup lukewarm water or milk
4 cups flour
1 tsp. salt
1 large egg

5 tbsp. melted butter

In a small bowl, add 2 packets of yeast and warm water then add t tsp. of sugar. Mix and wait for 5 minutes for yeast to activate.

In a stand mixer add 4 cups of flour, ¼ cup of sugar, 1 tsp. of salt, 1 large egg, and 5 tbsp. of butter. Slow mix the ingredients and then when yeast is ready, pour into the mixer bowl. Mix all ingredients until mixture sticks to the dough hook and makes a ball.

Sprinkle a little flour in the bowl, over the dough, and push the dough around before removing. Then remove dough and transfer to a greased bowl. Cover with plastic wrap, and allow it to rise in a warm place for one hour.

After dough has risen, punch it down and prepare to form balls from it.

Take two round cake pans, and line with aluminum foil. Then spray with cooking spray on the bottom and the sides.

Squeezing off round balls, make rolls about the size of the palm of your hand. Then twist the bottoms where you pinched them off, to keep them round, and place them into the cake pans. The ideal size of the balls would be around 7 to 8 balls in each pan.

Cover the baking pans with plastic wrap, and allow to rise for 25 to 35 minutes. Then brush with butter before placing into the oven.

Bake at 400 degrees for around 25 minutes or until golden brown. Brush with butter when they are done baking. Allow to sit 5 minutes before removing from pan.

Beer Rolls

Dissolve completely one packet of dry yeast in one cup of warm water. Place in large pan and add:
2 tbsp. sugar
1 slightly beaten egg
2/3 cup milk
1 tsp. salt
2 tbsp. melted shortening

Gradually add small amount of flour to this mixture until you have used about 4 1/2 cups. While adding the small amounts of flour also add 2 tbsp. of beer at a time until you have used 6 tbsp. of beer. Mix thoroughly after each addition. Do not use too much flour. When the dough is just dry enough to knead, and it should be slightly moist, knead until bubbles appear in the dough.

Then dip the entire batch of dough in melted butter, cover and let rise for 1 1/2 hours in a warm place.

Roll out dough and make rolls of your choice, parker house or clover leaf. Let rise in a warm place.

Bake in 475-degree oven until they are brown.
You had better keep a sharp eye on them because they bake quickly (the quicker, the better).

This makes about 30 parker house rolls or 18 clover leaf rolls.

Corn Pone

A standard pone recipe is:
1 cup corn meal
1 tsp. salt
3/4 cup boiling water
1 tablespoon lard or fat

Combine the corn meal and salt, while blending gradually add water. Melt the fat in the baking pan. After pan is greased, pour surplus into the mixture and blend.

The mix should not be more than one inch thick in the baking pan to start with. It will rise very little. (To make it rise like corn bread, 2 tsp of baking powder would be needed.) The pone will develop a rich, brown crunchy crust. In this modern day it would take about 50 to 60 minutes in a 350-degree oven.

Soft Pretzels

For **Pretzels**
1 tbsp. yeast
1 tbsp. sugar
1 tsp. salt
2 tbsp. soften butter or 2 tbsp. margarine
1 cup warm water (110 degrees)
2 3/4 cups flour
coarse salt

For **Baking Soda Boil**
5 teaspoons baking soda
4 cups water

Put yeast, sugar and water in bowl and stir. Let sit for 5 minutes and add salt, butter and 1 cup flour. Stir till smooth.

Add rest of flour and stir till mixed well. When mixture is too stiff to stir with a spoon (or you can use an electric mixer with dough hook), begin kneading. Knead dough till smooth and the dough no longer sticks to your hands. Place dough back in bowl and cover to rise to double its size.

While dough is rising, grease cookie sheet and preheat oven to 475°F Prepare baking soda boil by combining the 4 cups of water and 5 teaspoons baking soda in a non-aluminum pot and bring to a boil on stove.

When dough has risen, punch down and knead a minute or so. Divide and roll into 6-inch sticks to about 1/2-inch diameter with your hands, or 12-inch-long rolls to make into the pretzel shape.

Allow pretzels to sit for 2-3 minutes. Place 1-2 at a time into the boiling baking soda water.

Let pretzels boil for 1 minute and 10 seconds on one side, then flip them over and boil 1 minute and 10 seconds on the other side.

This boiling step is the secret to firm skin and adds that definite pretzel flavor. Not boiling them long enough leaves them too soft and allows them to rise too much. Boiling too long makes them tough. Err on the side of not too long if unsure.

Using a large slotted spoon, lift them out the of water, let them drip off and place on the greased cookie sheet. When all are done, sprinkle with coarse salt.

Bake 12-15 minutes until they are a medium to dark golden brown.

Makes 3 dozen 6-inch sticks or 1 dozen pretzels.

Corn Cakes

Fried on a griddle, these cakes were served with butter as bread or with sorghum molasses as pan cakes.

1 egg, beaten slightly
1 cup corn meal
1/2 cup flour
1 tsp. salt
1 cup hot water (or milk)
1 tablespoon fat or lard
1 tsp. sugar

Mix dry ingredients, then stir in the others. Drop or pour on hot, greased surface. Fry to a golden brown on both sides.

Southern Spoon Bread

Stir together:
1 cup yellow corn meal
1 1/2 tsp. baking powder
1/2 tsp. salt
In greased (one-quart size) casserole pour:
2 eggs (beaten)
2 tbsp. butter (melted)

In medium-sized pan heat:
2 1/4 cups milk (stir to avoid scorching)

As it starts boiling, sprinkle in the dry ingredients, stirring vigorously with wooden spoon. Cook and stir for 2 to 3 minutes, as it thickens, mix with eggs in casserole.

Bake at 425 degrees for 45 minutes. Serve from casserole with spoon. Add butter.

Keepsake Biscuit

1 quart milk or cream
1 1/2 cups butter or lard
2 tbsp. white sugar
1 good tsp. salt
1 tsp. cream of tarter
Enough flour to make stiff dough

Knead well and mold into neat, small biscuits with your hands. Bake well and you have a good, sweet biscuit that will keep for weeks in a dry place.

Potato Biscuits

1 cup mashed potatoes
2 tbsp. butter
1/2 tsp. soda
1 cup buttermilk
1 tbsp. honey
2 cups flour
2 tsp. baking powder
1 tbsp. brown sugar

Stir butter into potatoes. Dissolve soda in buttermilk, add honey. Mix baking powder, sugar, flour, adding in milk as you go. Press into 3/4" pad, cut biscuits. Bake at 400 degrees.

Buttermilk Biscuits

2 cups all-purpose flour
1 tablespoon baking powder
1/4 tsp. baking soda
1/2 tsp. salt
1/3 cup butter or margarine
3/4 to 1 cup buttermilk

Mix the flour together with the baking soda and salt, in a mixing bowl. Cut in the butter with a fork or 2 knives until the mixture is crumbly.

Stir in the ¾ cup of buttermilk all at once; add more buttermilk if needed to make a soft dough.

Knead the dough gently for about 5 minutes on a lightly floured board. Pat or roll dough about 1/2 thick; cut dough with a knife into squares.

Place biscuits on a baking sheet; brush tops with a little buttermilk. Bake in a preheated 450-degree oven 12 to 15 minutes, or lightly browned.

Parker House Rolls

1 cup scalded milk
1/4 cup sugar
1/4 cup butter
1/2 tsp. salt
1 package active dry yeast
2 cups sifted all-purpose flour
1/2 tsp. baking powder
1/2 tsp. baking soda
Melted butter or margarine

Pour the scalded milk over the sugar, butter, and salt; stir until butter is melted. Let the mixture cool to lukewarm then you can add the yeast.

Stir in the flour which has been sifted with the baking powder and soda. Let the dough rise until it has doubled in size.

Roll out on a floured board to 1/2" thickness; cut with round biscuit cutter. Then brush with melted butter and fold over.

Place them in a greased shallow pan, and let rise again. Bake in a preheated oven at 400 degrees for 15 minutes.

Whole Wheat Bread

2 cups scalded milk
1/3 cup molasses
2 tsp. salt
1 tablespoon yeast
1/4 cup warm water
4 2/3 cups whole wheat flour

Add molasses to milk. Let cool to luke-warm. Dissolve yeast in the luke-warm water. Put liquids together. Add them, as you stir, to the flour into which the salt has already been mixed. Beat well and cover. Let rise to double bulk. Again beat and turn into greased bread pans so that the pans are half full. Allow to rise in warm place until almost double. Bake at 400 degrees for about 50 minutes until it shrinks from the sides of the pans. Butter the top a few minutes before removing from oven.

Sour Dough Starter

2 cups flour
1 3/4 cups of warm water
6 tsp. dry yeast
2 tbsp. honey

Combine flour and dry yeast in a bowl. Mix honey in warm water and gradually add to dry ingredients. Store it in pot at room temperature for 2 days to one week.

Sour Dough Bread

The night before baking, combine one cup of starter (above) with 2 cups of warm water. Sift in 2 1/2 cups flour and beat well. Cover and leave 12 hours in warm place. (Then, before adding any other ingredients, return one cup of batter to the storage pot for future use.) Add enough flour to make stiff dough. Turn out onto lightly floured board; knead vigorously until smooth and elastic, about 10 minutes. Place in greased bowl. Place in warm place. Let it rest for 20 minutes. Form into loaves. Let rise until double. Bake at 400 degrees for about 25 minutes.

Apple Stuffing

Mix well but lightly; 7 cups bread crumbs; 3 cups apples, diced; 1 cup minced onion; 1 cup seedless raisins; 1 1/2 tsp. salt; 1 1/4 cup sugar; 1/2 cup melted butter; 1/4 tsp. pepper. Stuff and close bird. This makes enough for small turkey or goose. Bake according to pounds of fowl.

Oyster Stuffing

Cook 4 cups celery, diced fine, in 2 cups water until tender, about 18 minutes. Drain and save 1 cup liquid. Sauté 1/2 cup minced onions in ½ cup butter over low heat. Drain 1 1/2 cups of oysters. Add enough celery liquid to reserved oyster liquid to make 1 cup. Mix well 4 quarts lightly packed, day-old, dry bread crumbs with 2 tsp. poultry seasoning, 1 tablespoon salt, 1 tsp. pepper. Then combine dry ingredients with the liquid, onions, oysters, and blend well.

Corn Bread Stuffing

Simmer 1/4 cup minced onions in 1/2 cup butter in a large skillet until tender. Combine in a bowl: 1 1/2 quarts lightly packed cornbread crumbs, 3/4 tsp. salt, 1/2 tsp. poultry seasoning, 1 tsp. celery seed, 3 tbsp. minced parsley, and 1/8 tsp. pepper. Add to onion mixture and heat well without browning. Stir frequently. This recipe makes enough for a 4lb. bird.

Easy Mixer Bread

2 packages dry yeast
1/2 cup instant nonfat dry milk
2 tbsp. sugar
1 tablespoon salt
7 to 7 1/2 cups all-purpose flour
1/3 cup cooking oil
2 1/2 cups water (lukewarm)

Grease the bottom and sides of two 9"x5" loaf pans.

In a large mixer bowl, dissolve he yeast in the water. Add the dry milk, sugar, salt, and about 3 1/4 cups of the flour to the dissolved yeast.

Blend at low speed until moistened; beat 3 minutes at medium speed. By hand, gradually add remaining flour to form a very stiff dough. Cover, and let rest for 15 minutes.

Toss dough onto floured surface and knead until smooth, about 1 minute. Divide in half.

Using a rolling pin, shape the dough into a 12"x6" rectangle. Roll up tightly starting with 6" side. Seal edges and ends.

Place seam-side down in pans. Cover, let rise in warm place until doubled. Bake at 400 degrees for 30 to 35 minutes. Remove from the pans and cool on wire rack.

Corn Fritters

1 can chopped corn
1/2 cup sweet milk
1/2 cup flour
1 tsp. baking powder
1 tsp. salt
1 tsp. melted butter
2 eggs
Pepper to taste

Mix ingredients thoroughly. Drop the mixture by small spoonfuls into hot fat and fry until golden brown.

Fritters

1/4 cup onion (chopped)
1/4 tsp. salt
1/2 tsp. pepper
1 tsp. garlic (chopped)
1 cucumber
1 egg
1 cup flour
1 tsp. baking powder
1 tablespoon butter (melted)

Blend the first 5 ingredients together. Add the egg and mix thoroughly. Add the flour, baking powder, and butter and mix again. Drop by spoonfuls in hot fat. Cook until light brown.

Banana Nut Bread

1 1/2 cups mashed bananas
1 cup sugar
1 1/2 cups flour
1 tsp. baking soda
1 egg
1/2 cup cooking oil
1 tsp. vanilla
Nuts

Beat the egg with the sugar and oil. Then add the bananas, flour, baking soda, vanilla, and nuts. Pour into a bread pan and bake at 350 degrees for 1 hour.

Spiced Zucchini Bread

3 cups all-purpose flour
2 tsp. baking soda
1 tsp. salt
1/2 tsp. baking powder
1 1/2 tsp. ground cinnamon
3/4 cup walnuts (finely chopped)
3 eggs
2 cups sugar
1 cup vegetable oil
2 tsp. vanilla
2 cups coarsely shredded zucchini
1 (8 oz.) can crushed pineapple (well drained)

Combine the flour, baking soda, salt, baking powder, and nuts; set aside.

Beat the eggs lightly in a large mixing bowl; add the sugar, oil, and vanilla; beat until it becomes creamy. Stir in the zucchini and pineapple. Add the dry ingredients, stirring only until the dry ingredients are moistened.

Spoon the batter into 2 well-greased and floured 9"x5"x3" loaf pans. Bake them at 350 degrees for 1 hour or until it tests done. Let it cool for 10 minutes before removing them from the pans, turn out on rack and let cool completely.

Hush Puppies

1/2 cup all-purpose flour
2 tsp. baking powder
2 tbsp. powder
1/2 tsp. salt
1 1/2 cups cornmeal
1 egg (beaten)
3/4 cup milk
1 small onion (finely chopped)
Shortening for deep frying

Combine all the dry ingredients, and then add the egg and milk, mixing lightly. Stir in the chopped onion, if desired. Drop batter by teaspoonfuls into deep hot fat (360 degrees), frying only a few at a time. Cook until golden brown, and then drain on paper towel.

Cornbread

Sift the following ingredients together:
1 cup flour
3/4 tsp. baking soda
1 tsp. salt
1 tsp. baking powder
Add 1 1/2 cups cornmeal.

Combine the following ingredients together:
2 eggs (well beaten)
2 tbsp. brown sugar
1/2 cup melted shortening

Add the eggs, sugar, and shortening to 1 1/2 cups of buttermilk, then add to cornmeal mixture. Beat only until moist.

Bake in a well-oiled pan or iron skillet at 450 degrees until golden brown.

Easy Egg Bread

4 to 4 1/2 cups Bread Flour
1 (0.25oz) package (7g) or 2 1/4 teaspoons Red Star Active Dry Yeast
2 tbsps. granulated Sugar
2 tsps. table Salt
1/2 cup Water
1/2 cup Milk
2 tbsp. Shortening or butter
3 large Eggs (slightly beaten)
Egg wash: 1 egg yolk plus 1 teaspoon milk (whisked together)

In a stand mixer bowl, combine 2 cups flour, yeast, sugar and salt; mix well.

In saucepan or microwave-safe dish, heat water, milk and shortening/butter until warm (120-130°F; shortening/butter does not need to melt).

Add to flour mixture. Blend at low speed, slowly adding slightly beaten eggs – one at time, until fully incorporated; beat 3 minutes at medium speed.

Switch to dough hook attachment. Gradually stir in enough remaining flour to make a firm dough. Knead until smooth and elastic, about 5 to 8 minutes.

Place dough in lightly oiled bowl and turn to grease top. Cover; let rise until indentation remains after poking dough with finger down to second knuckle, about 1 hour.

Punch down dough. Divide into 3 parts. On lightly floured surface, roll each third to a 15-inch rope.

On greased cookie sheet loosely braid from center to ends. Pinch ends and tuck under to seal. Cover; let rise in warm place until indentation remains after lightly touching, about 30-45 minutes.

Preheat oven to 400°F.

Brush with egg wash. Bake for 25 to 30 minutes until golden brown. Remove from cookie sheet; cool on wire rack.

Cakes, Cookies, and Candy

Candy Coins

2 cups of sugar
1 cup of milk
1/2 cup of chopped nuts
1 pound chopped dates (about 2 1/2 cups)
1 cup shredded coconut

Combine sugar and milk in sauce pan. Cook over medium heat to a soft ball stage, stirring constantly.

Add dates. Cook, stirring constantly until mixture is very thick and will leave the sides of the pan when stirred.

Remove from heat. Stir in coconut and nuts. Cool just a little. Turn on wet towel.

When cool enough to handle and hold shape, roll in the towel. Place in refrigerator and chill.

Make a roll 2 inches in diameter (about 18 inches long). Wrap in wax paper. Freeze.

It will keep for about 6 months. To serve: let thaw to room temperature. Slice into thin rounds.

Ultimate Chocolate Chip Cookies

3/4 cup granulated sugar
3/4 cup packed brown sugar
1 cup butter or margarine, softened
1 teaspoon vanilla
1 egg
2 1/4 cups all-purpose flour
1 teaspoon baking soda

1/2 teaspoon salt
1 cup coarsely chopped nuts
1 package (12 ounces) semisweet chocolate chips (2 cups)

Heat oven to 375°F.

Mix sugars, butter, vanilla and egg in large bowl. Stir in flour, baking soda and salt (dough will be stiff). Stir in nuts and chocolate chips.

Drop dough by rounded tablespoonfuls about 2 inches apart onto ungreased cookie sheet.

Bake 8 to 10 minutes or until light brown (centers will be soft). Cool slightly; remove from cookie sheet. Cool on wire rack.

Chocolate Fudge

3 Cups of Dark Chocolate Chips (I sometimes substitute Belgium chocolate for about a third of the chocolate called for)
1 Can of Sweetened Condensed Milk
1 tsp of Vanilla Extract
1/2 cup of White Mini Marshmallows
1 cup of Chopped Walnuts (optional)

Combine chocolate, sweetened condensed milk and vanilla extract in a microwave safe bowl. Stir to coat the chocolate.

Microwave on high for about 2 minutes.

Stir occasionally, until all chocolate pieces have melted.

Stir in mini marshmallows until melted smooth. Pour into a pan. I use a glass dish lined with wax paper, so it is easy to pull out after cooling and cut the fudge.

Chocolate Chip Pecan Cookies

1 1/4 cups All Purpose Flour
1/8 tsp Salt
1/2 cup (1 stick) Butter, softened
1/3 cup Confectioner's Sugar
1/2 tsp Vanilla Extract
1/2 cup chopped Pecans
1/2 cup Milk Chocolate Chips

Preheat oven to 400 degrees.

In a large mixing bowl, cream together butter, brown sugar, and sugar for 4 minutes, or until light and fluffy. Scrape the sides of the bowl.

Add eggs and vanilla and mix for 1 minute longer.

Fold in cake flour, all-purpose flour, cornstarch, baking soda, and salt.

Fold in milk chocolate chips and pecans.
Place 5-ounce balls on light colored baking sheets.

Bake for 9-12 minutes or until light golden brown on the outside.

Remove from the oven and let sit for at least 10 minutes to allow the cookies to set up. Roll in powdered sugar.

Butterscotch Candy

Boil 2 cups brown sugar with 2 tsp. vinegar, 4 tsp. cold water and 1/2 cup butter until hard ball is formed when dropped in cold water. Pour in oiled pan.

Sea Foam

Dissolve 3 cups brown sugar and 1/4 tsp. salt in 3/4 cup water. Cook, without stirring, to hard ball stage. Pour gradually over 2 egg whites that have been beaten stiff. Beat constantly. Add I tsp. of vanilla and continue beating until cool. Drop by spoonful on wax paper.

Chocolate Fudge

2 cups sugar
2 squares chocolate
2/3 cups milk or water
2 tbsp. corn syrup
2 tbsp. butter

Combine and cook over low heat to 240 degrees. Remove and cool to 110 degrees. Add 1 tsp. of vanilla and beat. Spread on buttered dish or pan.

Heavenly Kisses

2 egg whites
1/2 tsp. vanilla
1/2 cup fine granulated sugar

Beat egg whites until stiff and dry, beat in 6 tbsp. of sugar, a spoon at a time. Beat until it forms peaks. Add vanilla, and then fold in the rest of the sugar. Shape with spoon on cookie sheet. Bake in 250-degree oven for 50 minutes. It makes about 18 to 20 kisses.

Milk and Honey Balls

1 1/4 cup honey
1 1/2 cups peanut butter
3 cups dry (powdered) skim milk

Mix honey and peanut butter. Gradually add dry milk, mixing well. With greased hands, form into small balls. Roll the balls in additional milk powder. Chill until firm.

Martha Washington Candy

2 cups sugar
1 cup water
2 tsp. butter
1/4 tsp. cream of tartar
1 tsp. vanilla

Mix the sugar, cream of tartar and water. Cook until it boils, do not stir. After it breaks in cold water, cool, add butter, when it is cold enough to beat. Beat until it crystallizes, knead and form into balls. Chopped nuts or raisins may be added. May be dipped in malted chocolate, to which a small amount paraffin wax has been added.

Nut Caramel Fudge

3 cups dark brown sugar
1 tsp. butter
1 1/2 cups of milk
1 tsp. vanilla
1 cup chopped nuts

Cook sugar, butter and milk until it will thread. Remove from heat. Add flavoring and nuts. Beat until mixture is thick and creamy. Pour in buttered pan. Cut into squares when cool.

Molasses Candy

2 cups molasses
1 cup sugar
1 tablespoon vinegar

Cook together until crunchy or brittle when dropped in cold water. Stir in a pinch of baking soda and three cups chopped black walnuts. Pour in greased pan. Break into pieces when cold.

Cocoa Drop Cookies

1/2 cup shortening
1 cup sugar
1 egg
3/4 cup buttermilk
1 tsp. vanilla
1 3/4 cups sifted flour
1/2 tsp. soda
1/2 tsp. salt

3 tbsp. cocoa
1/2 cup chopped nuts

Mix shortening, sugar, and egg together. Stir in the buttermilk and vanilla. Sift dry ingredients and stir in. Chill for one hour. Heat the oven to 400 degrees. Drop dough by teaspoonfuls, about 2 inches apart, on greased baking sheets. Bake 8 to 10 minutes, and frost with thin white icing.

Sour Cream Cookies

1/2 cup shortening
1 1/2 cups brown sugar
2 eggs
2 1/2 cups flour (sifted)
2/3 cup chopped walnuts
1/2 tsp. baking powder
1 tsp. soda
1/2 tsp. salt
1 cup thick sour cream
1 tsp. vanilla

Cream the shortening and sugar. Add eggs and mix thoroughly. Sift dry ingredients (about 1/3 of the dry ingredients) into the mixture, and alternate with the sour cream until both are used up. Add vanilla and nuts and blend. Drop by teaspoonfuls on greased cookie sheet. Bake at 350 degrees for about 12 minutes. This makes 6 dozen cookies. Frost with icing of a simple white variety or serve plain.

Applesauce Spice Cookies

1 3/4 cups flour
1/2 tsp. salt
1 tsp. cinnamon
1 cup sugar
1 cup applesauce
1 cup seedless raisins
1/2 tsp. cloves
1/2 tsp. nutmeg
1/2 cup shortening
1 egg
1 tsp. baking soda
1/2 cup rolled oats

Mix flour, salt, spices, and sift. Cream the sugar with shortening. Add beaten egg. Add mixed ingredients alternately with applesauce to creamed mixture, beating well. Stir in raisins and oats. Drop by teaspoonfuls, about 2 inches apart, onto a greased cookie sheet. Bake at 375 degrees for 10 to 15 minutes.

Spice Tomato Cake

1/2 cup butter
1 cup sugar
2 eggs
1/2 cup tomato sauce
1/2 tsp. vanilla
1/8 tsp. salt

Mix the above ingredients together thoroughly. Sift the following ingredients together and then add them to the above mixture, then bake at 350 degrees until it appears done.

1 tsp. baking powder

2 cups flour
1/2 tsp. cloves
1/2 tsp. nutmeg
1/2 tsp. cinnamon

Pork Cake

1-pint black coffee
1 lb. fresh mild sausage
1 box raisins
1 cup English walnuts
1 box dark brown sugar
1 tablespoon baking soda
1 tsp. cinnamon
1 tsp. all-spice
1 tsp. cloves
1 tsp. nutmeg
Enough flour to thicken

Put the sausage in pan to simmer until grease seeps out. Drain and add all the other ingredients. Bake it for 1 1/2 hours at 250 degrees.

Quick Caramel Frosting

1/2 cup butter
1/2 cup brown sugar (packed)
1 3/4 cups powdered sugar
1/2 cup sweet milk

Melt butter, add sugar, and boil for 2 minutes. Add sweet milk and stir until it comes to a boil. Remove from the heat, and let it cool. Add the powdered sugar and beat until right consistency to spread.

Delicious Pound Cake

3 sticks butter
1 stick margarine
2 cups sugar
3 cups flour
6 eggs
1/2 cup milk
1 tsp. baking powder
Pinch of salt
2 tbsp. lemon extract

Mix in order given and bake at 325 degrees for 1 hour and 25 minutes, or until the cake comes away from the sides.

Old Fashioned Stack Cake

4 eggs
1/2 cups butter
2 cups sugar
1 cup milk
1 tsp. vanilla
1/4 tsp. salt
3 tsp. baking powder
4 cups flour
3 lbs. dried apples (sliced)

Cream the butter and the sugar until they are creamy. Add the eggs and beat. Add the milk, vanilla, salt, baking powder, and flour (a little bit at a time until stiff enough to roll out). Pinch off dough and roll on a floured board, until about 1/4" thick. Use a small plate to cut it out, and bake on top of stove in un-greased skillet until brown. This makes about 20 cakes or layers. Cook the apples until they are soft, then you can sweeten and mash them. Put the cake layers together with the apples, a layer of apples on each cake; leave the top layer without apples. Best if stored for 2 to 3 days until eaten.

Burnt Sugar Cake

2 cups sifted cake flour
2 tsp. baking powder
1/4 tsp. baking soda
1/4 tsp. salt
1/2 cup butter
1 cup sugar
1 egg (beaten slightly)
1 egg yolk
1 cup cold water
1 1/2 tbsp. burnt sugar syrup

Mix and sift the flour, baking powder, baking soda, and salt. Cream the butter and the sugar. Add egg and yolk. Beat until smooth and light. Add alternately water with dry ingredients. Add burnt sugar syrup. Pour into 2 greased and floured 9" pans. Bake at 350 degrees for 25-30 minutes, and then frost with the burnt sugar syrup.

Note: To make burnt sugar syrup, heat 1/4 cup sugar, stir constantly in heavy skillet. When melted add 1/4 cup hot water and stir until dissolved, and let cool.

Burnt Sugar Icing

2 egg whites
1 1/2 cup sugar
Dash of salt
1/3 cup water

144

2 tsp. dark corn syrup
2 tbsp. burnt sugar syrup

Combine the egg whites, sugar, water, and corn syrup in top of double boiler. Heat some water to boiling point. Beat with beater for about 7 minutes or until mixture thickens and holds shape. Remove from boiling water, and add burnt sugar syrup and continue to beat until stiff enough to spread.

One Minute Fudge Icing

2 squares unsweetened chocolate
2 cups white sugar
1/2 cup sweet milk
1/2 cup butter

Melt chocolate, add ingredients. Boil for 1 minute. Set off heat and beat until spreading consistency.

Fruit Cake

4 cups flour
3 cups sugar
1 lb. butter
10 eggs
1-quart shelled pecans
1 lb. white raisins
1 tsp. baking powder
1 tsp. mace
1 tsp. vanilla
1/2 lb. red candied cherries
1/2 lb. green candied cherries
1/2 lb. red candied pineapple

1/2 lb. green candied pineapple

Cream the butter, flour, mace, and baking powder together. Beat the eggs and add sugar. Add this mixture to the butter and flour and mix well. Add chopped fruits, nuts, and raisins. Mix thoroughly. Bake at 275-300 degrees for about 2 hours. This makes ten pounds.

Hickory Nut Cake

1/2 cup butter and shortening (about half and half)
1 tsp. vanilla
2 cups cake flour
1 cup chopped hickory nuts
2 tsp. baking powder
1/4 tsp. salt
1/4 cup milk
4 egg whites (beaten stiff)

Cream the butter, sugar, and vanilla until fluffy. Sift flour, baking powder, and salt. Add alternately with the milk to creamed mixture. Beat until smooth. Fold in nuts and egg whites. Pour into 2 greased 8x8x2 pans. Bake at 350 degrees for 35 minutes. Cool. Before serving put layers together and frost with sweetened whipped cream. Sprinkle with chopped hickory nuts.

Hard-Times Cake

Mix 1/2 cup of butter, 2 cups sugar, 1 cup sour cream, 3 cups flour, 3 eggs, and 1/2 tsp. baking soda. Bake in layers at 350 degrees and spread with jelly.

Chocolate Potato Cake

2 cups flour
2 tsp. baking powder
1 tsp. cinnamon
1/2 tsp. nutmeg
1 1/2 cups sugar
1/2 cup raisins
1 cup mashed potatoes
1/2 cup melted chocolate (unsweetened)
3/4 cup milk
1 cup chopped nuts
1/2 cup butter

Sift the dry ingredients 3 times. Cream the butter and sugar until they are fluffy, and then add the dry ingredients to this mixture, alternating with the milk. Add nuts and raisins after mixing in the mashed potatoes and melted chocolate. Blend well. Bake in 2 buttered or lined 8x8 pans in 350-degree oven for about 35 minutes.

Blueberry Tea Cake

1/3 cup shortening
2 cups flour
2 tsp. baking powder
1 cup blueberries
1/4 tsp. salt
1 cup sugar
3/4 cup milk
1 egg

Fresh or frozen berries may be used for this cake. Be sure to drain the berries before using in the cake mixture. Remove any old berries and stems from fresh berries.

Stir the shortening to soften. Add the flour, which has been
sifted with the baking powder, salt, and sugar and mix
thoroughly. Then add the milk. Beat vigorously at least 2
minutes. Add the eggs and beat for 1 minute. Stir in the
blueberries carefully. Pour into greased 8x8x2 cake pan.
Bake in 350-degree oven for about 50 minutes.

Lemon Sauce (for Blueberry Tea Cake)

1/4 cup sugar
1 tablespoon corn starch
1 cup water
Dash of salt
3 tbsp. lemon juice
1 tsp. lemon rind
1 tsp. butter

Mix together the sugar, corn starch, and salt. Stir in the
water and lemon juice until mixture is smooth. Add grated
lemon rind. Cook over moderate heat until thick and clear.
Stir often. Remove from heat and add butter, stir until
melted.

This can also be used to dress up pound cake or any other
plain desserts.

Frosted Brownies
2 3/4 cups flour
1/2 tsp. salt
2 1/2 tsp. baking powder
2/3 cup shortening (part butter)
1/4 tsp. red food coloring, nuts or raisins
2 1/2 cups brown sugar
3 eggs

3 tbsp. cocoa

Melt shortening in large sauce pan. Add sugar, and then add eggs one at a time. Stir. Add sifted dry ingredients. Then add nuts and raisins. Bake at 350 degrees for about 25 minutes, when cool add frosting below.

Milk Chocolate Frosting

Beat together 2 cups powdered sugar, 4 tbsp. butter, 3 level tbsp. of cocoa, 1 tsp. vanilla and enough cream for easy spreading.

Yummy Oatmeal Cookies

1 cup shortening
3/4 tsp. salt
1 tsp. cinnamon
1/2 tsp. cloves
1 1/2 cups brown sugar
2 eggs (beaten)
1 1/2 cups rolled oats (not quick oats)
1/2 cup chopped nuts
1 cup raisins
2 cups flour
1/4 cup buttermilk
3/4 tsp. baking powder

Cream the shortening, salt, spices, and brown sugar together. Add beaten eggs and mix well. Add rolled oats, nuts, and raisins. Sift flour and baking powder, and then mix the dry ingredients alternately with buttermilk. Drop by teaspoonfuls onto greased baking sheet. Bake at 350 degrees. This can make 6 dozen cookies.

Walnut Wafers

2 eggs, 1/2-pound brown sugar, 4 tbsp. flour, 1/4 tsp. baking powder, 1/3 tsp. salt, 1/2-pound black walnuts (chopped). Beat eggs, add all other ingredients. Drop by tsp. on greased cookie sheet and bake at 325 degrees until you can stick a fork into them and it comes out clean.

Ginger Cookies

1 egg, 1 cup sugar, 1 cup molasses, 1 tablespoon baking soda, 1 tablespoon of vinegar, 1 tablespoon of ginger, 2 or more cups of flour, enough to stiffen. Mix and roll thin. Cut into small cookies and bake at 350 degrees for about 10 minutes.

Jumbo Drops

1 cup shortening
2 cups brown sugar
3 eggs
1/2 cup water
1 tsp. vanilla
3 1/2 cups sifted flour
1/2 tsp. salt
1 tsp. baking soda
1/4 tsp. cinnamon

Heat the oven to 375 degrees. Mix the shortening, sugar, and eggs together thoroughly. Stir in water and vanilla. Sift and stir in flour, baking soda, salt and cinnamon. Drop by tsp. onto greased baking sheet. Place ½ tsp. filling on dough, cover with ½ tsp. dough. Bake 10 to 12 minutes.

Filling – Cook together until thick 2 cups dates cut into small pieces, 3/4 cup sugar, 1/4 cup water. Add 1/2 cup chopped nuts. Chill before using.

Carrot Cake

4 eggs
2 cups white sugar
2 tsp. baking soda
3 cups grated carrots
1 1/2 cups cooking oil
2 cups flour
2 tsp. cinnamon

Mix all together thoroughly. Bake at 300 to 325 degrees until done, and let cool.

Frosting – Cream 8oz. package of softened cream cheese with 1/2 lb. butter, 1 lb. powdered sugar, 2 tsp. vanilla, and 1 cup chopped nuts.

Grandma's Jam Cake

1 cup butter
2 cups blackberry jam
2 cups sugar
3 cups flour
1 tsp. baking soda
1 cup buttermilk
1 tsp. cloves
1 tsp. nutmeg
1 tsp. cinnamon
3 eggs

Cream shortening and sugar together, then add eggs and the blackberry jam. Beat together thoroughly. Sift the flour, measure and resift with baking soda, salt, and spices. Add alternately with milk to the first mixture. Beat well. Pour into greased tube cake pan. Bake at 350 degrees for about 55 minutes. For the topping use the caramel frosting recipe.

Cherry Nut Cake

1/2 cup shortening
2 1/2 cups flour
1 1/2 cups sugar
1 tsp. salt
3 tsp. baking powder
1 tsp. vanilla
2 tsp. almond
1/4 cup milk
1/4 cup maraschino juice
4 egg whites (beaten)
1 cup maraschino cherries
1 cup chopped pecans

Cream shortening and sugar together, then add beaten egg whites. Mix dry ingredients and add them to the creamy mixture. Add cherry juice to the milk and add alternately with the dry ingredients. Add cherries and nuts. Bake at 350 degrees for 1 hour. Use whatever frosting you wish.

Black Walnut Pound Cake

1 lb. powdered sugar
3/4 lb. butter
6 large eggs
1 tsp. vanilla

1 tsp. black walnut extract
1 cup chopped black walnuts (chopped)
3 cups + 2 tbsp. flour

Cream the butter and sugar until light. Add and beat in one egg at a time. Add flour one third at a time. Add vanilla and walnut extract. Fold in the black walnuts. Bake in tube pan. Pan should be greased or lined on the bottom with brown paper. Bake 1 hour and 20 minutes at 350 degrees, and let cool for about 10 minutes before removing from the pan.

Poor Man's Fruit Cake

Combine in 2 cups raisins, 2 cups hot water, and 3/4 cup lard in sauce pan. Cook for five minutes, boil rapidly but don't let it burn. Set aside. Sift together 3 1/2 cups flour with 2 tbsp. baking soda, 2 tsp. cinnamon, 1 tsp. nutmeg, 1/2 tsp. cloves. Add to first mixture, now cooled. Stir in 1 jar assorted fruits and candied fruit peels. 1 cup nuts may be added. Turn into a greased and floured tube or loaf pan and bake for 2 hours at 275 degrees.

Golden Icing

1/4 cup butter
1/4 tsp. salt
2 egg yolks
1/3 cup cream
1/4 tsp. almond extract
1/4 tsp. vanilla
6 cups sifted powdered sugar

Cream the butter with the salt and egg yolks. Add sugar alternately with cream. Mix. Add extracts. Add cream if it is too thick.

Apple Dapple Cake

Cream 3 eggs with 1 1/2 cups cooking oil, and 2 cups sugar. Sift together and fold in: 3 cups flour, 1 tsp. salt, 1 tsp. baking soda, and 2 tsp. of vanilla. Blend and add 1 cup chopped peeled cooking apples.

Bake at 350 degrees for about 45 minutes in a 9x13x2 pan. Leave it in the pan. Add this topping: 1 cup brown sugar, 1 stick butter, and 1/4 cup milk. Boil 2 1/2 minutes and pour over hot cake. Let it cool in the pan. Some of the topping will be absorbed and make the cake moist and delicious.

Children's Delight

Cook 2 cups raisins in 1 cup water for 5 minutes. Cream 1 cup lard with 2 cups sugar. Add 3 beaten eggs, 1 tsp. vanilla, and cool cooked raisins.

Sift together 4 cups flour, 1 tsp. baking powder, 1 tsp. baking soda, 1 tsp. cinnamon, 1/2 tsp. salt. Add sifted ingredients to the above mixture.

Drop by small teaspoonfuls about 1 1/2" apart on a greased cookie sheet. Bake at 350 degrees for 12 to 15 minutes. Remove from pan immediately. This makes about 4 dozen.

Frozen Lemon Cream

1 egg (well beaten)
1/4 cup lemon juice
1/8 tsp. salt
1 tsp. lemon peel (grated)
1/4 cup butter (melted)
2 drops food coloring (yellow)
1 cup whipped cream
1/2 cup brown sugar
Pinch of nutmeg
1/2 cup nuts (chopped)
3 cups bite-sized toasted corn cereal (crushed to 3/4 cup)
1 tsp. vanilla
3/4 cup grated coconut

Line the bottom and sides of a loaf pan with wax paper.
Extend the paper over the rim of the pan.

Combine egg, lemon juice, sugar, salt, and lemon peel.
Heat in top of double boiler until mixture coats a spoon.

Cook 12 to 15 minutes over hot water but not boiling water.
Remove from heat, and stir in vanilla and food coloring.
Cool thoroughly.

Combine the butter, brown sugar, and nutmeg. Add nuts
and corn cereal crumbs. Mix until evenly blended. Save ¾
of the crumb mixture for topping.

Press remaining crumbs into prepared pan. Fold the
coconut and whipped cream into the lemon cooled mixture,
then spoon into pan. Top with reserved crumbs.

Press crumbs together lightly. Cover and freeze for at least
6 hours or overnight. This will make 8 servings.

Nut Crescents

Mix together by hand the following ingredients: 1 cup butter (or margarine), 1/2 cup confectionery sugar, 2 cups sifted flour, 2 tsp. vanilla, and 1 cup chopped pecans. Shape into balls or crescents. Bake 20 minutes at 350 degrees.

Butter Cookies

Cream 1/2 cup butter, 1/2 cup shortening, and 3/4 cup sugar until fluffy. Add 1 beaten egg and 2 tsp. vanilla. Sift together 3 cups flour, 1/2 tsp. baking powder, and 1/8 tsp. salt. Add this to cream mixture very gradually. Roll out on a pastry cloth and cut into desired shapes. A cookie press may be used. Bake at 375 degrees until light brown.

Holiday Macaroons

Beat 2 eggs until fluffy. Add slowly 3/4 cup sugar and beat until thickened...about 5 minutes. Sift together 1/3 cup flour, 1/4 tsp. baking powder, 1/8 tsp. salt, and add to above mixture. Then add 1 tablespoon melted butter, 1 tsp. vanilla, 1 tsp. grated lemon rind, and 2 2/3 cups flaked coconut. Drop by teaspoonfuls onto greased and floured baking sheets. Decorate with cherry, nuts, or sugar sprinkles.

Bake at 325 degrees for 15 minutes. Cool completely. Store tightly.

Almond Bark Candy

2 lb. almond bark
3 cups peanuts
3 cups Captain Krunch cereal
1/2 cup peanut butter
2 cups Rice Krispies
2 cups miniature marshmallows

Melt the almond bark in a double boiler and stir in peanut butter. Pour over the remaining ingredients. Mix and drop by spoonfuls on wax paper.

Uncooked Chocolate Fudge

3 squares unsweetened chocolate (melted)
1/2 cup oleo (softened)
1 lb. powdered sugar
1 egg (beaten)
1 cup nuts (finely chopped)
1 tsp. vanilla

Melt the chocolate and oleo together. Mix the sugar and the egg thoroughly, and then add the chocolate mixture and vanilla. Mix thoroughly. Stir in the nuts. Spread in an oiled 8"x9" pan. Chill for at least 2 hours, and then cut into squares.

Pumpkin Cake with Cream Cheese Frosting

4 eggs
2 cups sifted all-purpose flour
2 tsp. baking soda
1/2 tsp. salt

1 tsp. ground cloves
2 tsp. ground cinnamon
1/2 tsp. ginger
1/2 tsp. nutmeg
2 cups sugar
1 cup salad oil
1 lb. can of pumpkin
Pecan or walnut halves (as needed)

In a large bowl of electric mixer, let the eggs warm to room temperature, about 30 minutes.

Preheat the oven to 350 degrees.

Sift the flour with baking soda, salt, cloves, cinnamon, ginger, and nutmeg.

Beat the eggs at high speed with sugar until light and fluffy.

Beat in the oil and pumpkin and blend thoroughly.

At low speed, beat in the flour mixture until just combined.

Pour into an un-greased 9" tube pan. Bake for 1 hour or until fork comes out clean. Cool completely in pan.

With spatula, carefully loosen from pan. Frost with Cream Cheese Frosting (below), and decorate with nuts.

Cream Cheese Frosting

2 – 3oz. packages cream cheese (softened)
1 tablespoon rum or 1 tsp. vanilla extract
3 cups powdered sugar

In a medium bowl, with electric mixer at medium speed, beat cheese with rum until cream. Gradually beat in sugar, until light and fluffy. Spread over Pumpkin Cake (above), making swirls with knife.

Brandy Bourbon Fruitcake

15 oz. box seedless raisins
8 oz. chopped candied cherries
8 oz. box chopped dates
1 pint bourbon
1 cup brandy
5 cups flour
1 tsp. baking powder
2 tsp. nutmeg
1 1/2 cups butter
1 cup brown sugar
2 cups white sugar
6 egg yolks
6 eggs whites (beaten)
1 cup walnuts (chopped)
1 cup almond slices

Soak the raisins, cherries, and the dates in the bourbon and brandy overnight (1 week is better) in a glass jar covered in refrigerator.

Mix and sift the flour with the baking powder and the nutmeg.

Cream the butter with the brown sugar and white sugar. Add the egg yolks and beat well. Add the soaked fruit liquid and then the fruit, alternating with the flour. Add the egg whites. Fold in the walnuts and almond slices. Mix thoroughly.

Line a 7" tube pan with greased brown paper.

Bake at 275 degrees for 4 hours and 15 minutes.

Remove from the oven. Pour wine over the hot cake while cooling in the pan.

Remove from the pan. Wrap in wine-soaked cheese cloth, then wrap in wax-coated freezer paper.

Store it in a cool place. <u>Do not use foil.</u> The liquor will eat up the foil.

Gingerbread

1/2 cup sugar
½ cup butter and shortening mixed (about ½ and ½)
1 egg (beaten)
1 cup molasses (dark is best)
2 1/2 cups flour
1 1/2 tsp. baking soda
1 tsp. cinnamon
1 tsp. ginger
1/2 tsp. cloves
1/2 tsp. salt
1 cup hot water

Cream the sugar with the butter and shortening mixture. Add the egg and molasses. Sift the flour, baking soda, cinnamon, ginger, cloves, and salt together. Add to the creamed mixture. Add 1 cup of hot water and beat until smooth. Bake in a greased shallow pan for 35 minutes at 325 to 350 degrees. Serve hot with butter or whipped cream.

Doughnuts

(makes about 2 dozen)
3 eggs
1 cup sugar
1/2 cup margarine (melted)
1 cup milk
About 4 cups all-purpose flour
3 tsp. baking powder
1/4 tsp. salt
About 5 cups oil (for deep frying)
Powdered sugar (optional)

Beat the eggs until they are very light. Then add the sugar, and beat until the mixture becomes thick and creamy. Next you add the margarine and milk and mix thoroughly. Sift the 3 cups of flour with the baking powder and salt, and then add this to the batter. Add just enough flour to make a dough that can be rolled; roll the dough to ½" thickness. Next you can cut out the doughnuts using a doughnut cutter. Heat the oil to 375 degrees, and <u>gently</u> add the doughnuts, a few at a time. Fry the doughnuts, turning twice, until golden; drain on paper towels. Finally while the doughnuts are still warm you can sprinkle the powdered sugar over them.

Funnel Cakes (Drechter Kuche)

3 eggs
2 cups milk
1/4 cup sugar
3 to 4 cups flour
1/2 tsp. salt
2 tsp. baking powder
Beat the eggs, and add the sugar and milk.

Sift the flour with the salt and baking powder, and then add this to the egg mixture.

Beat the batter smooth and add only as much flour as needed. The batter should be thin enough to run through a funnel. Drop from the funnel into deep, hot fat (375 degrees).

Spirals and endless intricate shapes can be made by swirling and criss-crossing while controlling the funnel spout with a finger. Serve hot with molasses, tart jelly, jam, or sprinkle with powdered sugar.

Honey Oatmeal Cookies

2 tbsp. butter (room temperature)
1 tablespoon oil
1/2 cup brown sugar
1/4 cup honey
1 egg
1 tablespoon water
1/2 cup flour
1/2 tsp. salt
1/4 tsp. baking soda
1 1/2 cups quick rolled oats
Fruits, nuts, or chocolate bits (optional)

Grease cookie sheets and set aside. Preheat the oven to 350 degrees. Blend the butter, oil, brown sugar, honey, egg, and water thoroughly. In another bowl, mix the flour, salt, and baking soda together. Stir and blend the two mixtures together. Add the fruits, nuts, or chocolate bits (if desired). Drop by teaspoonfuls onto the prepared cookie sheets, and bake at 350 degrees for 10 to 12 minutes.
This recipe makes 3 dozen cookies.

Texas Sheet Cake

Sift the following together in a large bowl:
2 cups sugar
2 cups all-purpose flour
1/2 tsp. salt
Bring the following to a boil:
2 stick margarine
1 cup water
4 tbsp. cocoa

In a small bowl mix 2 eggs (beaten), 1 tsp. baking soda, 1 tsp. white vinegar, 1 tsp. vanilla, and 1/2 cup buttermilk. Mix all the previous mixtures together in a large bowl, beat well, and pour into a greased 17"x11"x1" pan. Bake at 350 degrees for 30 minutes.

Frosting:
Bring the following ingredients to a boil:
1 stick margarine
4 tbsp. cocoa
6 tsp. milk or buttermilk
1 tsp. vanilla

Remove it from the heat and add 1 box powdered sugar and a dash of salt. Beat until it becomes smooth. Then pour over the while hot. Let the icing firm a little before serving.

Holiday Rum Balls

3 cups crushed vanilla wafers
1 cup powdered sugar
3 tbsp. corn syrup
1 1/2 tbsp. cocoa
1 cup walnuts (chopped)

3oz. rum

Work all the ingredients together. A few drops of hot water may be added so the mixture will stick together. Pinch off small pieces and roll into balls. Roll them in additional powdered sugar. Store them in a covered container for a day or so before serving.

Walnut Bourbon Balls

2 1/2 cups finely crushed vanilla wafers
1 cup powdered sugar
2 tbsp. cocoa
1 cup walnuts (finely chopped)
1 cup coconut (optional)
3 tbsp. corn syrup
1/4 cup bourbon
Powdered sugar

Mix the wafers, sugar, cocoa, nuts, and coconut together thoroughly. Add the corn syrup and the bourbon; mix thoroughly. Pinch off pieces and roll into 1" balls, and roll in powdered sugar.

7 Up Cake

Mix 1 box of yellow cake mix according to the directions on the box, and to this add 1 package (3 oz.) of vanilla instant pudding and 4 eggs. Beat this until it becomes smooth then add; 10oz. of 7 Up soda. Blend and bake at 350 degrees for 30 to 35 minutes.

Icing: To make the icing combine 2 eggs (beaten) with 1 1/2 cups of sugar, 1 stick margarine, and 1 tablespoon flour. Mix thoroughly and add 1 cup crushed pineapple (un-drained). Cook until it becomes thick, and then add 1 can of coconut (shredded). Pour over the hot cake and serve.

Mound Candy

1/3 cup mashed white potatoes
1/3 cup powdered sugar
2 ¾ cups coconut
½ tsp. vanilla
1 bag chocolate chips
Small piece of paraffin wax

Combine the potatoes, sugar, coconut, and vanilla and shape into small balls. Refrigerate. Melt the chocolate chips and wax together. Dip the cool balls into the chocolate. Place them on waxed paper until the chocolate is firm.

Pumpkin Bread

1 3/4 cups all-purpose flour
1 1/2 cups sugar
1 tsp. baking soda
1 tsp. cinnamon
1 1/2 tsp. salt
1/2 tsp. nutmeg
1/8 tsp. cloves
1/2 cup melted butter
1 cup pumpkin
1 egg (beaten)
1/3 cup water

Sift all the dry ingredients together, and then make a well in the center. Add all the other ingredients (mixed together) to the dry ingredients. Mix until it is moistened.

Pour this mixture into a greased and floured loaf pan. Bake for 1 hour and 10 minutes at 350 degrees. Let cool and remove from the pan.

Pumpkin Layer Cheesecake

2 packages cream cheese (softened)
1/2 cup sugar
1/2 tsp. vanilla
2 eggs
1/2 cup canned pumpkin
1.2 tsp. ground cinnamon
Dash of cloves
Dash of nutmeg
1 ready-to-use graham cracker crumb crust (9")

Mix the cream cheese with the sugar and vanilla with an electric mixer on medium speed until well blended. Next you can add the eggs, mix until blended thoroughly.

Next you want to stir the pumpkin and spices into 1 cup of the batter; pour the remaining plain batter into the crust.

Then top with the pumpkin batter.

Bake it at 375 degrees for 35 to 40 minutes or until center is almost set. Let cool then refrigerate for 3 hours or overnight.

This recipe makes about 8 servings.

Bourbon Balls

1/2 cup butter
1 cup powdered sugar
4 tbsp. bourbon
1 cup finely chopped pecans
1 large package semisweet chocolate chips
1 tablespoon paraffin

Cream the butter with the sugar, and then add the bourbon with the pecans. Shape into small balls and place on waxed paper. Refrigerate for at least 30 minutes. Melt the chocolate chips; add paraffin. Dip the balls into the chocolate, and then let sit to harden.

Chocolate Vanilla Swirl Cheesecake

20 Oreo cookies (crushed, about 2 cups)
3 tbsp. butter (melted)
4 packages (8 oz. each) cream cheese (softened)
1 cup sugar
1 tsp. vanilla
1 cup sour cream
4 eggs
6 squares semi-sweet baking chocolate (melted, cooled)

Preheat the oven to 325 degrees, and line a 13"x9" pan with foil, with ends of foil extending over sides of pan.

Mix the cookie crumbs with the butter, and then press firmly onto the bottom of the prepared pan. Bake this for 10 minutes.

Beat the cream cheese together with the sugar and vanilla in a large bowl with an electric mixer on medium speed until it is well blended. Add the sour cream and mix again. Add the eggs; one at a time, beating at low speed after each addition just until blended.

Remove 1 cup of the batter; set aside.

Stir the melted chocolate into the remaining batter in a large bowl; pour over the crust. Top this with spoonfuls of the remaining 1 cup plain batter; cut through the batters with a knife several times for swirling effect.

Bake this for 40 minutes or until center is almost set. Let it cool. Then refrigerate at least 4 hours or overnight. Use the foil handles to lift the cheesecake from the pan before cutting to serve. Store any leftover cheesecake in the refrigerator.

This recipe makes about 16 servings.

Peanut Butter Fudge

1 cup brown sugar
1 cup sugar
1/2 cup evaporated milk
2 tbsp. butter
1 cup marshmallows
3/4 cup peanut butter
1 tsp. vanilla

Combine the sugar, milk, and butter in a heavy saucepan; cook to soft-ball stage, 235 degrees on a candy thermometer. Add the remaining ingredients; stir until the marshmallows melt. Remove from the heat and beat until the mixture begins to thicken, about 1 minute. Pour this into a buttered 8" square pan and let cool. Cut into serving pieces.

This recipe will yield about 1 ½ lbs. of fudge.

Boston Cream Pie

3 eggs (beaten)
1 cup sugar
1 cup sifted
1 tsp. baking powder
2 tbsp. milk

Chocolate Velvet Cake

1 – 6 oz. package semisweet chocolate morsels
2 1/4 cups sifted flour
1 tsp. baking soda
3/4 tsp. salt
1 3/4 sugar
3/4 cup softened butter
1 tsp. vanilla
3 eggs

Combine the chocolate morsels together with ¼ cup water in saucepan. Stir over a low heat until it is melted and smooth. Remove it from the heat. Sift the flour, baking soda, and slat together and set aside. Combine the sugar, butter, and vanilla in a bowl. Beat until they are blended thoroughly. Add the eggs, 1 at a time, beating well after each addition. Blend in the melted chocolate mixture. Stir in the flour mixture alternately with 1 cup water. Pour into 2 greased and floured 9" layer cake pans. Bake these at 375 degrees for 30 to 35 minutes. Then let them cool.

Chocolate Velvet Frosting

1 – 6 oz. package semisweet chocolate morsels
3 tbsp. butter
1/4 cup milk
1 tsp. vanilla
3 cups sifted powdered sugar

Melt the chocolate morsels and butter over a hot, not boiling, water. Remove from the water, and add the milk, vanilla, and salt. Mix until they are thoroughly blended. Next beat in the powdered sugar, gradually. Fill and frost the Chocolate Velvet Cake.

Fruit Cocktail Cake

2 cups flour
2 cups white sugar
2 tsp. baking soda
2 eggs
13 oz. can fruit cocktail
1 tsp. vanilla

Combine all the ingredients, and mix thoroughly. Bake in a 9"x13" pan at 350 degrees for 35 minutes.

Topping – Combine 1 1/2 cups of brown sugar, 1 small can or cup of cream, 1/2 stick of butter, 1 cup of coconut, and some nuts, making sure to mix thoroughly. Cook at 350 degrees for 10 minutes, and then spread on cake.

Dump Cake

1 (21 oz.) can cherry pie filling
1 (21 oz.) can crushed pineapple
1 box yellow cake mix
2 sticks melted margarine
1 can of coconut
1 cup chopped pecans

Put in a pan in the order given. <u>Do not stir or mix.</u>
Bake at 325 degrees for 1 hour.

Strawberry Soda-Pop Cake

1 box white cake mix
2 small boxes of strawberry Jell-o
1 can or small bottle strawberry soda
1 1/2 cups hot water
1 small box vanilla instant pudding
1 small carton Cool Whip

Prepare the white cake mix according to the directions on the box. Bake in a 10"x13" cake pan. As soon as you take it out of the oven, while hot, prick holes all over the top and let cake cool completely.

Mix the 2 boxes of strawberry Jell-o with the hot water and soda, dissolve the Jell-o thoroughly. Pour the mixture over the cake. Chill until the cake is set and firm.

Mix the pudding with milk and heat until thick. Fold in Cool Whip and spread on cake. Keep refrigerated.

Peanut Butter Balls

1 lb. powdered sugar
1 stick butter
12 oz. creamy peanut butter
1 bar chocolate coating (melted)

Blend the sugar, butter, and peanut butter together.
Roll into balls and dip into the melted chocolate coating.
Place on rack and refrigerate to harden.

Dirt Cake

1 1/4 lbs. Oreos (crushed)
2 small packages vanilla instant pudding
8 oz. cream cheese
12 oz. Cool Whip
3 1/2 cups milk
1/2 stick butter
1 cup powdered sugar

Crush the Oreos in a food processor. They can also be
crushed in a plastic freezer bag with a rolling pin or bottom
of glass. Mix the pudding with milk. Refrigerate. Mix the
cream cheese with the butter and powdered sugar. Mix the
pudding with the Cool Whip, and then combine with the
cream cheese mixture. Layer crumbs with the pudding,
starting and ending with Oreo crumbs. Chill for about 12
hours. Layer in a foil-lined flower pot, and add plastic
flowers and gummy worms. Use a new trowel to serve.

No Bake Cookies

2 cups sugar
1/2 cup milk
1/2 cup cocoa
1 stick butter
1/4 tablespoon salt
1/2 cup peanut butter
1/2 cup pecans or other nuts
3 cups oatmeal
1 tsp. vanilla

Combine the milk, sugar, butter, and cocoa in a saucepan; boil for 1 minute (after it starts boiling). Remove it from the stove and quickly add the peanut butter, oatmeal, nuts, and vanilla. Mix thoroughly and drop by a tsp. onto waxed paper.

Grandma's Sugar Cookies

2 cups flour
1/2 tsp. baking soda
1/4 tsp. salt
1/4 tsp. nutmeg
1/4 tsp. lemon flavoring
1/2 cup butter
3/4 cup sugar
1/2 cup sour cream

Sift together the first five ingredients, and let it stand for a while. Cream the butter and sugar together. Then blend in the sour cream and dry ingredients, mixing thoroughly. Let chill. Roll out the dough on a floured surface, half of the dough at a time, to 1/8" thickness. Cut into desired shapes and place on un-greased cookie sheets and bake.

Bake at 350 degrees for 8 to 10 minutes.

This recipe makes about 6 to 7 dozen.

Oatmeal Carmelites

Base:
2 cups all-purpose flour
2 cups quick-cooking oats
1 1/2 cups brown sugar
1 1/4 cups butter (softened)
1 tsp. baking soda
1/2 tsp. salt

Filling:
1 jar (12.25 oz.) caramel ice cream topping
3 tbsp. all-purpose flour
1 cup semisweet chocolate chips
1/2 cup chopped nuts

Heat the oven to 350 degrees, and grease a 13"x9" pan with shortening or spray. In a large bowl beat the base ingredients with an electric mixer on low speed until crumbly. Reserve half of the crumb mixture (about 3 cups) for topping. Press the remaining crumb mixture in the bottom of the pan. Bake this for 10 minutes. Meanwhile, in a small bowl, stir the caramel topping with the 3-tbsp. flour. Sprinkle the chocolate chips and nuts over partially baked base. Drizzle evenly with the caramel mixture, sprinkle with the reserved crumb mixture. Bake for 18 to 22 minutes longer or until golden brown. Let cool completely in the pan on cooling rack, about 1 hour. Refrigerate 1 to 2 hours or until filling is set. If you want bars, cut it into 6 rows by 6 rows. Keep stored in a tightly covered container.

Granny's Sour Cream Pound Cake

1 cup butter (softened)
2 3/4 cups sugar
6 eggs
3 cups sifted all-purpose flour
1/2 tsp. salt
1/2 tsp. vanilla extract
1/2 tsp. almond extract
1/4 tsp. baking soda
1 cup sour cream

Cream the butter in a large bowl until it becomes fluffy. Add the sugar and beat until it become light and fluffy. Add the eggs, one at a time, beating thoroughly after each addition. Sift the flour and salt together 3 times. Add the vanilla extract and the almond extract. Next add the baking soda to the sour cream. Add the dry ingredients alternately with the sour cream, mixing well after each addition. Pour into a greased and floured tube pan. Bake at 350 degrees for 1 hour and 20 minutes. Let it cool and then remove from the pan.

Red Velvet Cake

1/2 cup butter
1 1/2 cups sugar
2 eggs
2 oz. red food coloring
2 tbsp. cocoa
1 cup buttermilk
2 1/4 cups sifted cake flour
1/2 tsp. salt
1 tsp. baking soda
1 tsp. vinegar

Cream the butter with the sugar, and then add the eggs. Make paste of food coloring and cocoa; add to creamed mixture. Stir in buttermilk alternately with flour and salt, and then add the vanilla. Add the baking soda to the vinegar; fold over bowl as this mixture foams; add, blending instead of beating.

Place batter in 2 greased and floured 8" pans. Bake at 350 degrees for 25 to 30 minutes.

Red Velvet Cake Frosting

9 tbsp. cake flour
2 cups milk
1 cup sugar
1 cup shortening
1 tsp. vanilla

Cook the flour and milk together until very thick, cook completely. Cream the sugar, shortening, and vanilla until very light and fluffy. Add this to the flour mixture. Mix until very well blended; it should be texture of whipped cream.

Frost the top and sides of each layer, and then stack

Potato Pinwheel Candy

2 boxes powdered sugar
1 small potato (cooked, peeled, and mashed)
1 tsp. vanilla
2 tsp. butter (melted)
1 medium jar of peanut butter

Put the sugar into a large bowl, and then add the vanilla and melted butter. Add the mashed potato, a little at a time, working until you have a soft dry ball.

Roll out into rectangle about 3/8" thick. Spread the peanut butter over top of the candy. Starting with the long side of the rectangle, roll to make a cylinder-shaped tube.

Pinch both sides together to seal, and slice 1/2" thick. Place between layers of wax paper and chill until serving time.

Peanut Brittle

1 cup sugar
1/3 cup light corn syrup
1 cup raw peanuts
2 tbsp. + 2 tsp. water
2/3 tsp. baking soda
Dash of salt

In a heavy saucepan, stir together the sugar, corn syrup, and water. Cook over a medium heat, stirring constantly, until the sugar is dissolves and comes to a boil. Cook without stirring to 280 degrees (soft crack stage). Then add the peanuts and stir often and watch closely until it reaches 300 degrees (hard crack stage). Remove from heat and add baking soda.

Pour into a large greased cookie sheet. As it cools, stretch a little. Cool enough, and then break.

Peanut Butter Chews

1 cup peanut butter
1 cup Karo syrup
1 cup sugar
1 1/4 cup corn flakes

Bring the sugar and syrup to a boil. Then stir in the peanut
butter and corn flakes. Drop by tsp. onto waked paper.

Chocolate Pound Cake

5 oz. package unsweetened chocolate
3/4 cup milk
1/4 cup strong black coffee
1/2 cup butter
3 cup sugar
5 eggs
2 1/2 cups flour
1 tsp. baking powder
1/2 tsp. salt
1/4 tsp. cinnamon
1 tsp. brandy
Powdered sugar as needed

Melt chocolate with the milk and coffee, and set aside to
cool. In a large bowl, cream the butter until it's light and
fluffy. Gradually add the sugar, 1/4 cup at a time, mixing
constantly until thoroughly blended. Beat in the eggs, one
at a time for 3 minutes. Stir together flour, baking powder,
salt, and cinnamon. Add the brandy to the cooled chocolate
mixture. Add the dry ingredients and the chocolate mixture
to the butter mixture alternatively, blending well after each
addition. Butter a 10" tube pan. Line the bottom with wax
paper and butter. Bake it at 325 degrees for about 1 ½ hours

or until cake tests done. Let the cake cool in the pan. Turn onto a rack and carefully peel off paper. Sprinkle with powdered sugar.

Pie Crust

2 cups flour
1 cup shortening
1 tsp. salt
1/3 cup milk
1 tsp. vinegar

Mix the flour with the salt and shortening. Then mix the vinegar with the milk and add this to the flour mixture. Knead and roll out on floured board. This makes two large crusts.

Rolled Oats Cookies

3 cups quick oats
2 1/2 cups flour
2 tsp. cinnamon
1 tsp. baking soda
1 tsp. salt
1 1/2 cups sugar
2 eggs
3/4 cup milk
1 cup oil
1 cup raisins
1 cup walnuts (chopped)
1 cup carrots (finely grated)

Mix the oats, flour, cinnamon, baking soda, salt, and sugar together thoroughly. Add the well-beaten eggs, milk, and oil. Stir thoroughly. Add the raisins, nuts, can carrots. Mix and drop by spoonfuls on greased cookie sheets.

Sugar Cookies

1 cup shortening
1 cup butter or margarine
1 cup powdered sugar
1 cup granulated sugar
2 eggs
Pinch of salt
1 tsp. vanilla
4 cups flour
1 tsp. baking soda
1 tsp. cream of tarter

Beat the shortening, butter, and sugars together until they get fluffy. Add the remaining ingredients and mix well. Refrigerate for 3 or 4 hours. Form into balls the size of a walnut and roll in sugar and press flat on un-greased cookie sheet. Bake at 350 degrees for 10 minutes.

Toasted Coconut Cookies

Blend a 1/2 cup of shortening, 1 cup of sugar, 1/2 cup butter, and 1 egg. Then add 2 cups of sifted flour, 1/2 tsp. of baking soda, 1/2 cup cream of tartar, 1 tsp. vanilla, and 1 cup toasted coconut. Chill and roll into balls, and then press onto a greased cookie sheet. Bake at 350 degrees for 10 to 14 minutes.

Peanut Butter Cookies

1/2 cup butter
1/2 cup peanut butter
1/2 cup white sugar
1/2 cup brown sugar
1 egg (beaten)
1/4 cup flour
1 tsp. baking soda

Cream the butter with the peanut butter. Add the sugars and cream thoroughly. Blend in the egg. Sift the flour and baking soda together and work into creamed mixture. Form into balls and flatten on a baking sheet with a fork. Bake at 350 degrees for 10 minutes.

Chocolate Chip Cookies

3 3/4 cups flour (white or whole wheat)
1 1/2 tsp. baking soda
1 1/2 tsp. salt
1 1/2 cups white sugar
3/4 cup brown sugar
3 eggs
3 tsp. vanilla
1 1/2 cups shortening
12 oz. bag of chocolate chips

Blend the flour, baking soda, salt, sugars, eggs, vanilla, and shortening together and mix for 1 minute. Stir in the chocolate chips. Drop batter by the tsp. on an un-greased cookie sheet. Bake at 375 degrees for 10-12 minutes. This makes about 120-130 cookies.

'Hurry Up' Cookies

2 cups sugar
1/4 cup margarine
1/2 tsp. salt
1/4 cup cocoa
1/2 cup milk

Mix all the above in a saucepan. Bring to a boil, stir, and boil for 1 1/2 minutes.

Quickly stir in:

2 cups minutes oats   1 tsp. vanilla
1/2 cup peanut butter   1/2 cup raisins, nuts, or
                                              coconut (optional)

Stir until the mixture begins to thicken. Drop on wax paper by spoonfuls. Let set a few minutes while the cookie sets up. This makes about 2 1/2 dozen cookies.

Peanut Butter Cake

Prepare 1 package of yellow cake mix as directed except – before blending, add 1 cup crunchy or creamy peanut butter. Frost the cake with Peanut Butter Frosting (below).

Peanut Butter Frosting

3 cups powdered sugar
1/4 cup crunchy peanut butter
1/4 to 1/3 cup milk

Mix the sugar and peanut butter; stir in the milk. Beat until it's at spreading consistency.

Pumpkin Bread

3 cups white sugar
1 cup Crisco
4 eggs
3 1/2 cups flour
1 tsp. nutmeg
1 tsp. vanilla
1 tsp. salt
2/3 cup water
2 cup pumpkin
1 tsp. cinnamon
2 tsp. baking soda

Mix all the ingredients together, and pour into greased bread pans. Bake at 350 degrees for 1 hour or until a toothpick comes out clean. This recipe can make 3 loaves.

Sauerkraut Cake

2/3 cup shortening
1 1/2 cup sugar
3 eggs (beaten)
1 tsp. vanilla
2 1/2 cups flour
1/2 cup cocoa
1 tsp. baking soda
1 tsp. baking powder
1/2 tsp. salt
1 cup water
1 cup sauerkraut (drained)

Mix the shortening, sugar, eggs, and vanilla together. Sift the flour, and then re-measure with the cocoa, baking soda, baking powder, and salt. Add water and sauerkraut. Mix thoroughly. Bake in a square pan at 350 degrees until done.

Fudge Sheet Cake

2 cups flour
2 cups granulated sugar
3 sticks butter or margarine
8 tbsp. cocoa
1 cup water
1/2 cup buttermilk
2 tsp. vanilla
1 tsp. baking soda
2 eggs
6 tbsp. sweet milk
Dash of salt
1 box powdered sugar

Mix the flour and the sugar in a large bowl. In a saucepan, combine 2 sticks of butter or margarine, 4 tbsp. cocoa, and water and bring to a boil. Cool for 1 minute. Pour over the flour mixture, and then add the buttermilk, 1 tsp. of the vanilla, baking soda, and eggs. Beat the mixture until smooth, for about 1 minute. Pour into greased, floured pan. Bake for 30 minutes at 325 degrees. Five minutes before the cake is taken from the oven, combine remaining butter, vanilla, cocoa, sweet milk, and dash of salt in saucepan and bring to a boil. Remove from heat and add powdered sugar. Spread over the cake while it's still hot.

Helpful Hints

How to Avoid Food Poisoning
In Home-Cooked Foods

Proper cooking and handling of food can reduce the risk of food poisoning. Salmonella and other bacteria can be present in meat and poultry products without giving off any telltale signs, like bad taste or bad smell, so it's important to prevent these bacteria from spreading or multiplying to dangerous levels. The basic rule is: keep hot foods hot and cold foods cold. Here are some recommendations for avoiding trouble:

- Don't thaw meat or poultry on the kitchen counter. Instead, thaw it overnight in the refrigerator, or put frozen package in a watertight plastic bag under cold water, changing the water often.

- Don't leave hot food out for more than two hours. Even in a chafing dish, the food often isn't kept hot enough to discourage bacteria growth.

- Don't cool leftovers on the kitchen counter. It's safer to put them straight into the refrigerator.

- Pick up perishable foods last when grocery shopping, and get them home and into the refrigerator quickly.

- Repeated handling can introduce bacteria into food. Leave food in the original store wrapper when refrigerating.

- Keep your refrigerator set at 40 degrees or lower.

Cook meat and poultry thoroughly to kill bacteria. Most food poisoning bacteria are killed at cooking temperatures between 165 degrees and 212 degrees. Use a meat thermometer, instead into the thickest part, away from the bone or fat.

Freeze Now – Heat Later

One of the best things about modern times that the good old days lacked is refrigeration, and the convenience of cooking food ahead of time, freezing it, and then being able to just heat it up when we need it. Here are some tips on using your freezer to keep foods tasting delicious and staying fresh:

- Always chill dishes freezing them, since a still-warm dish takes longer to freeze and allows the formation of ice crystals that change the color, taste, and texture of the food.

- Ceramic, metal, or glass baking dishes may be used to freeze prepared foods if they are tightly covered. Use packaging materials that are moisture proof, reasonably airtight, and durable. Heavy aluminum foil, freezer paper or bags, poly wrap, and strong plastic containers protect foods from freezer burn.

- Leave about half an inch of space (especially for foods with a sauce) so foods will have room to expand while freezing. When storing food in bags, press out excess air before sealing.

- Before you freeze, label each package with the contents, date prepared, and the number of servings.

- Don't freeze emulsified sauces such as hollandaise sauce; they will curdle and separate. Cream sauces are also risky to freeze, and gelatin or whipped-cream desserts don't freeze successfully.

- Be sure that your freezer is cold enough. Frozen foods held at 0 degrees or lower retain their quality longer.

Suggested Maximum Home-Storage Periods to Maintain Good Quality in Purchased Frozen Foods

Food	Approximate holding period at 0 degrees Fahrenheit

Fruits and Vegetables

	Months
Fruits, fruit juice concentrates	12
Vegetables	8

Baked Goods

Bread and yeast rolls:	
White Bread	3
Cinnamon Rolls	2
Plain Rolls	3
Cakes:	
Chocolate layer	4
Pound or Yellow	6
Fruit	12
Pies (unbaked):	
Apple and other fruit	8

Meat

Beef:	
Hamburger	4
Roasts and Steaks	12
Lamb:	
Patties (ground meat)	4
Roasts	9
Pork, cured:	2
Pork, fresh:	
Chops	4
Roasts	8
Veal:	
Cutlets, chops, and roasts	9
Cooked meat:	
Meat dinners and pies	3

Suggested Maximum Home-Storage Periods to Maintain Good Quality in Purchased Frozen Foods

Food	Approximate holding period at 0 degrees Fahrenheit

Poultry

	Months
Chicken:	
Cut-up	9
Whole	12
Duck or goose, whole:	6
Turkey:	
Cut-up	6
Whole	12
Cooked chicken or turkey dinners:	6

Fish and Shellfish

Fish Fillets:	
Cod, Flounder, Haddock, Halibut, Pollack	6
Mullet, Ocean Perch, Sea Trout, Striped Bass	3
Salmon steaks	2
Whiting, drawn	4
Shellfish:	
Clams, shucked	3
Oysters, shucked	4
Crabmeat:	
Dungeness	3
King	10
Shrimp:	12
Cooked fish and shellfish:	3

Frozen Desserts

Ice Cream or Sherbet	1

Cooking Tips

1. After stewing a chicken, cool in broth before cutting into chunks; it will have twice the flavor.
2. To slice meat into thin strips, as for stir-fry dishes, partially freeze it so it will slice more easily.
3. A roast with the bone in it will cook faster than a boneless roast. The bone carries the heat to the inside more quickly
4. When making a roast, place a dry onion soup mix in the bottom of your roaster pan. After removing the roast, add 1 can of mushroom soup and you will have good brown gravy.
5. For a juicier hamburger, add cold water to the beef before grilling (1/2 cup to 1 lb. of meat).
6. To freeze meatballs, place them on a cookie sheet until frozen. Place in plastic bags. They will stay separated so that you may remove as many as you want.
7. To keep cauliflower white while cooking, add a little milk to the water.
8. When boiling corn, add sugar to the water instead of salt. Salt will toughen the corn.
9. To ripen tomatoes, put them in a brown paper bag in a dark pantry, and they will ripen overnight.
10. To keep celery crisp, stand it upright in a pitcher of cold, salted water and refrigerate.
11. When cooking cabbage, place a small tin cup or a can half full of vinegar on stove near the cabbage. It will absorb the odor.
12. Potatoes soaked in salt water for 20 minutes before baking will bake more rapidly.
13. Let raw potatoes stand in cold water for at least a half-hour before frying in order to improve the crispness of French-fried potatoes. Dry potatoes thoroughly before adding to oil.

14. Use greased muffin tins as molds when baking stuffed green peppers.
15. A few drops of lemon juice in water will whiten boiled potatoes.
16. Buy mushrooms before they "open". When stems and caps are attached firmly, mushrooms are truly fresh.
17. Do not use metal bowls when mixing salads. Use wood, glass, or china.
18. Lettuce keeps better if you store it in the refrigerator without washing it. Keep the leaves dry. Wash lettuce the day you are going to use it.
19. Do not use baking soda to keep vegetables green. It destroys Vitamin C.
20. Do not despair if you over-salt gravy. Stir in some instant mashed potatoes to repair the damage. Just add a little more liquid in order to offset the thickening.
21. A leaf of lettuce dropped into the pot absorbs the grease from the top of soup.   Remove the lettuce and throw it away as soon as it has served its purpose.
22. To prevent splashing when frying meat, sprinkle a little salt into the pan before putting in the fat.
23. When bread is baking, a small dish of water in the oven will help to keep the crust from getting hard.
24. Rinse a pan in cold water before scalding milk to prevent sticking.
25. When you are creaming butter and sugar together, it's a good idea to rinse the bowl with boiling water first. They'll cream faster.
26. Dip the spoon in hot water to measure shortening, butter, etc.; the fat will slip out more easily.
27. Using a can opener that leaves a smooth edge, remove both ends from a flat can (the size that tuna is usually packed in) and you have a perfect mold for poaching eggs.
28. When preparing to bake biscuits, use the divider from an ice tray. Shape the dough to conform to the size of

the try, and press divider on dough. After baking the biscuits will separate at dividing lines.

29. Try using a thread instead of a knife when a cake is to be cut while it is still hot.

30. For lump-less gravies and creamy smooth sauces, use a small spring whisk and stir till all ingredients are blended.

Herbs & Spices

Acquaint yourself with herbs and spices. Add in small amounts, ¼ tsp. for every 4 servings. Crush dried herbs or snip fresh ones before using. Use 3 times more fresh herbs if substituting fresh for dried.

Basil – Sweet, warm flavor with an aromatic odor. Use whole or ground. Good with lamb, roast, stews, ground beef, vegetables, dressing and omelets.

Bay Leaves – Pungent flavor. Use whole leaf but remove before serving. Good in vegetable dishes, seafood, stews and pickles.

Caraway – Spicy taste and aromatic smell. Use in cakes, breads, soups, cheese and sauerkraut.

Chives – Sweet, mild flavor like that of onion. Excellent in salads, fish, soups and potatoes.

Cilantro – Use fresh. Excellent in salads, fish, chicken, rice, beans and Mexican dishes.

Curry Powder – Spices are combined to proper proportions to give a distinct flavor to meat, poultry, fish, and vegetables.

Dill – Both the seeds and leaves are flavorful. Leaves may be used as garnish or cooked with fish, soup, dressings, potatoes, and beans. Leaves or the whole plant may be used to flavor pickles.

Fennel – Sweet, hot flavor. Both the seeds and leaves are used. Use in small quantities in pies and baked goods. Leaves can be boiled with fish.

Ginger – A pungent root, this aromatic spice is sold fresh, dried or ground. Use in pickles, preserves, cakes, cookies, soups, and meat dishes.

Marjoram – May be used either dried or green. Use to flavor fish, poultry, omelets, lamb, stew, stuffing, and tomato juice.

Mint – Aromatic with a cool flavor. Excellent in beverages, fish, lamb, cheese, soup, peas, carrots, and fruit desserts.

Oregano – Strong, aromatic odor. Use whole or ground in tomato juice, fish, eggs, pizza, omelets, chili, stew, gravy, poultry, and vegetables.

Paprika – A bright red pepper, this spice is used in meat, vegetables, and soups or as a garnish for potatoes, salads, or eggs.

Parsley – Best when used fresh, but it can be used dried as a garnish or as a seasoning. Try in fish, omelets, soup, meat, stuffing, and mixed greens.

Rosemary – Very aromatic. It can be used either fresh or dried. It can be used to season fish, stuffing, beef, lamb, poultry, onions, eggs, bread, and potatoes. Great in dressings.

Saffron – Orange-yellow in color, this spice flavors or colors foods. Use in soup, chicken, rice, and breads.

Sage – Use either fresh or dried. The flowers are sometimes used in salads. May be used in tomato juice, fish, omelets, beef, poultry, stuffing, cheese spreads and breads.

Tarragon – Leaves have a pungent, hot taste. Use to flavor sauces, salads, fish, poultry, tomatoes, eggs, green beans, carrots, and dressings.

Thyme – Sprinkle leaves on fish or poultry before broiling or baking. Throw a few sprigs directly on coals shortly before meat is finished grilling.

Baking Breads
Hints for Baking Breads

1. Kneading the dough for 30 seconds after mixing improves the texture of baking powder biscuits.
2. Instead of shortening, use cooking or salad oil in waffles and hot cakes
3. When bread is baking, a small dish of water in the oven will help keep the crust from hardening.
4. Dip a spoon in hot water to measure shortening, butter, etc., and the fat will slip out more easily.
5. Small amounts of leftover corn may be added to pancake batter for variety.
6. To make bread crumbs, use the fine cutter of a food grinder and tie a large paper bag over the spout in order to prevent flying crumbs.
7. When you are doing any sort of baking you get better results if you remember to preheat your cookie sheet, muffin tins or cake pan.

Rules for Use of Leavening Agents

1. In simple flour mixtures, use 2 tsp. baking powder to leaven 1 cup flour. Reduce this amount by ½ tsp. for each egg used.
2. To 1 tsp. baking soda use 2 ¼ tsp. cream tarter, 2 cups freshly soured milk, or 1 cup molasses.
3. To substitute baking soda and an acid for baking powder, divide the amount of baking powder by 4. Take that as your measure and add acid according to rule 2.

Proportions of Baking Powder to Flour

Biscuits.. To 1 cup flour use 1 ¼ tsp. baking powder

Cake with oil.. To 1 cup flour use 1 tsp. baking powder

Muffins... To 1 cup flour use 1 ½ tsp. baking powder

Popovers... To 1 cup flour use 1 ¼ tsp. baking powder

Waffles.. To 1 cup flour use 1 ¼ tsp. baking powder

Proportions of Liquid to Flour

Drop Batter....................................	To 1 cup liquid use 2 to 2 ½ cups flour
Pour Batter....................................	To 1 cup liquid use 1 cup flour
Soft Dough....................................	To 1 cup liquid use 3 to 3 ½ cups flour
Stiff Dough....................................	To 1 cup liquid use 4 cups flour

Baking Breads
Time and Temperature Chart

Breads	Minutes	Temperature (degrees)
Biscuits......	12-15	......................400 – 450
Cornbread......	25-30	......................400 – 425
Gingerbread.....	40-50	......................350 – 370
Loaf.............	50-60	......................350 – 400
Nut Bread......	50-75	350
Popovers.......	30-40	......................425 – 450
Rolls.........	20-30	......................400 - 450

Baking Desserts
Perfect Cookies

Cookie dough that is to be rolled is much easier to handle after it has been refrigerated for 10 to 30 minutes. This keeps the dough from sticking, even though it may be soft. If not done, the soft dough may require more flour and too much flour makes cookies hard and brittle. Place on a floured board only as much dough as can be easily managed. Flour the rolling pin slightly and roll lightly to desired thickness. Cut shapes close together and add trimmings to the dough that needs to be rolled. Place pans or sheets in upper third of oven. Watch the cookies carefully while baking in order to avoid burned edges. When sprinkling sugar on cookies, try putting it into a salt shaker in order to save time.

Perfect Pies

1. Pie crust will be better and easier to make if all the ingredients are cool.
2. The lower crust should be placed in the pan so that it covers the surface smoothly. Air pockets beneath the surface will push the crust out of shape while baking.
3. Folding the top crust over the lower crust before crimping will keep juices in the pie.
4. In making custard pie, bake at a high temperature for about 10 minutes to prevent a soggy crust. Then finish baking at a low temperature.
5. When making cream pie, sprinkle crust with powdered sugar in order to prevent it from becoming soggy.

Perfect Cakes

1. Fill cake pans 2/3 full and spread batter into the corners and sides, leaving a slight hollow in the center.
2. Cake is done when it shrinks from the sides of the pan or if it springs back when touched lightly with the finger.
3. After removing a cake from the oven, place it on a rack for about 5 minutes. Then, the sides should be loosened and the cake turned out a rack in order to finish cooling.
4. Do not frost cakes until thoroughly cool.
5. Icing will remain where you put it if you sprinkle cake with powdered sugar first.

Baking Desserts
Time and Temperature Chart

Dessert	Time	Temperature (degrees)
Butter cake, layer....	20-40 min.	..........380 – 400
Butter cake, loaf......	40-60 min.	..........360 – 400
Cake, angel............	50-60 min.	..........300 – 360
Cake, fruit............	3-4 hrs.	..........275 – 325
Cake, sponge.........	40-60 min.	..........300 – 350
Cookies, molasses...	18-20 min.	..........350 – 375
Cookies, thin.........	10-12 min.	..........380 – 390
Cream Puffs...........	45-60 min.	..........300 – 350
Meringue..............	40-60 min.	..........250 – 300
Pie Crust..............	20-40 min.	..........400 - 500

Vegetables & Fruits

Vegetables	Cooking Method	Time
Artichokes	boiled	40 min.
	steamed	45 – 60 min.
Asparagus, tips	boiled	10 -15 min.
Beans, lima	boiled	20 – 40 min.
	steamed	60 min.
Beans, string	boiled	15 -35 min.
	steamed	60 min.
Beets, old	boiled or steamed	1 – 2 hrs.
Beets, young with skin	boiled	30 min.
	steamed	60 min.
	baked	70 – 90 min.
Broccoli, flowerets	boiled	5 – 10 min.
Broccoli, stems	boiled	20 – 30 min.
Brussels, sprouts	boiled	20 – 30 min.
Cabbage, chopped	boiled	10 – 20 min.
	steamed	25 min.
Carrots, cut across	boiled	8 – 10 min.
	steamed	40 min.
Cauliflower, flowerets	boiled	8 – 10 min.
Cauliflower, stem down	boiled	20 – 30 min.
Corn, green, tender	boiled	5 – 10 min.
	steamed	15 min.
	baked	20 min.
Corn on the cob	boiled	8 – 10 min.
	steamed	15 min.
Eggplant, whole	boiled	30 min.
	steamed	40 min.
	baked	45 min.

Parsnips	boiled	25 – 40 min.
	steamed	60 min.
	baked	60 – 75 min.
Peas, green	boiled or steamed	5 – 15 min.
Potatoes	boiled	20 – 40 min.
	steamed	60 min.
	baked	60 – 75 min.
Pumpkin or Squash	boiled	20 – 40 min.
	steamed	45 min.
	baked	60 min.
Tomatoes	boiled	5 – 15 min.
Turnips	boiled	25 – 40 min.

Vegetables & Fruits
Drying Time Table

Fruits	Sugar or Honey	Cooking Time
Apricots...................	¼ cup for each cup of fruit	..............About 40 min.
Figs...........................	1 tablespoon for each cup of fruit	..............About 30 min.
Peaches....................	¼ cup for each cup fruit	..............About 45 min.
Prunes.....................	2 T. for each cup of fruit	..............About 45 min.

Buying Fresh Vegetables

Artichokes: Look for compact, tightly closed heads with green, clean-looking leaves. Avoid those with leaves that are brown or separated.

Asparagus: Stalks should be tender and firm; tips should be close and compact. Choose the stalks with very little white; they are more tender. Use asparagus soon because it toughens rapidly.

Beans, Snap: Those with small seeds inside the pods are best. Avoid beans with dry-looking pods.

Broccoli, Brussels Sprouts, and Cauliflower: Flower clusters on broccoli and cauliflower should be tight and close together. Brussels sprouts should be firm and compact. Smudgy, dirty spots may indicate pests or disease.

Cabbage and Head Lettuce: Choose heads that are heavy for their size. Avoid cabbage with worm holes and lettuce with discoloration or soft rot.

Cucumbers: Choose long, slender cucumbers for best quality. May be dark or medium green, but yellow ones are undesirable.

Mushrooms: Caps should be closed around the stems. Avoid black or brown gills.

Peas and Lima Beans: Select pods that are well-filled but not bulging. Avoid dried, spotted, yellow, or flabby pods.

Buying Fresh Fruits

Bananas: Skin should be free of bruises and black or brown spots. Purchase them green and allow them to ripen at home at room temperature.

Berries: Select plump, solid berries with good color. Avoid stained containers which indicate wet or leaky berries. Berries with clinging caps, such as blackberries and raspberries, may be unripe. Strawberries without caps may be overripe.

Melons: In cantaloupes, thick, close netting on the rind indicates best quality. Cantaloupes are ripe when the stem scar is smooth and the space between the netting is yellow or yellow-green. They are best when fully ripe with fruity odor.

Honeydews are ripe when the rind has a creamy to yellowish color and velvety texture. Immature honeydews are whitish-green.

Ripe watermelons have some yellow color on one side. If melons are white or pale green on one side, they are not ripe.

Oranges, Grapefruit, and Lemons: Choose those heavy for their size. Smoother, thinner skins usually indicate more juice. Most skin markings do not affect quality. Oranges with a slight greenish tinge may be just as ripe as fully colored ones. Light or greenish-yellow lemons are more tart than deep yellow ones. Avoid citrus fruits showing withered, sunken or soft areas.

Measurements & Substitutions

Measurements

A pinch	1/8 tsp. or less
3 tbsp.	1 tablespoon
4 tbsp.	¼ cup
8 tbsp.	½ cup
12 tbsp.	¾ cup
16 tbsp.	1 cup
2 cups	1 pint
4 cups	1 quart
4 quarts	1 gallon
8 quarts	1 peck
4 pecks	1 bushel
16 ounces	1 pound
32 ounces	1 quart
1 ounce liquid	2 tbsp.
8 ounce liquid	1 cup

**Use standard measuring spoons and cups.
All measurements are level.**

Substitutions

Ingredient	Quantity	Substitute
Baking Powder	1 tsp.	¼ tsp. baking soda plus ½ tsp. cream of tarter
Ketchup or Chili Sauce	1 cup	1 cup tomato sauce plus ½ cup sugar and 2 tbsp. vinegar (for use in cooking)
Chocolate	1 square (1oz.)	3 or 4 tbsp. plus 1 tbsp. butter
Cornstarch	1 tbsp	2 tbsp. four or 2 tsp. quick tapioca
Cracker Crumbs	¾ cup	1 cup bread crumbs
Dates	1 lb.	1 ½ cup dates, pitted and cut
Dry Mustard	1 tsp.	1 tbsp. prepared mustard
Flour, Self-Rising	1 cup	1 cup all-purpose flour, ½ tsp. salt, and 1 tsp. baking powder
Herbs, Fresh	1 tbsp.	1 tsp. dried herbs
Milk, Sour	1 cup	1 tbsp. lemon juice or vinegar plus sweet milk to make 1 cup (let stand for 5 minutes)
Milk, Whole	1 cup	½ cup evaporated milk plus ½ cup water
Mini Marshmallows	10	1 large marshmallow
Onion, Fresh	1 small	1 tbsp. instant minced onion
Sugar, Brown	½ cup	2 tbsp. molasses in ½ cup granulated sugar
Sugar, Powdered	1 cup	1 cup granulated sugar plus 1 tsp. cornstarch

Tomato Juice	1 cup	½ cup tomato sauce plus ½ cup water

Equivalency Chart

Food	Quantity	Yield
Apple	1 medium	1 cup
Banana, mashed	1 medium	1/3 cup
Bread	1 ½ slices	1 cup soft crumbs
Bread	1 slice	¼ cup fine, dry crumbs
Butter	1 stick or ¼ lb.	½ cup
Cheese, American, cubed	1 lb.	2 2/3 cups
Cheese, American, grated	1 lb.	5 cups
Cheese, Cream Cheese	3 oz. package	6 2/3 tbsp
Chocolate, bitter	1 square	1 oz.
Cocoa	1 lb.	4 cups
Coconut	1 ½ lb. package	2 2/3 cups
Coffee, ground	1 lb.	5 cups
Cornmeal	1 lb.	3 cups
Cornstarch	1 lb.	3 cups
Crackers, Graham	14 squares	1 cup fine crumbs
Crackers, Saltine	28 squares	1 cup fine crumbs
Egg	4-5 whole	1 cup
Egg, Whites	8 – 10	1 cup
Egg, Yolks	10 – 12	1 cup
Evaporated Milk	1 cup	3 cups whipped
Flour, Cake, sifted	1 lb.	4 ½ cups
Flour, Rye	1 lb.	5 cups
Flour, White, sifted	1 lb.	4 cups
Flour, White un-sifted	1 lb.	3 ¾ cups
Gelatin, flavored	3 ¼ oz.	½ cup
Gelatin, unflavored	¼ oz.	1 tbsp.
Lemon	1 medium	3 tbsp. juice
Marshmallows	16	¼ lb.
Noodles, cooked	8 oz. package	7 cups
Noodles, uncooked	4 oz. (1 ½ cups)	2 – 3 cups cooked
Noodles, Macaroni, cooked	8 oz. cooked	6 cups
Noodles, Macaroni, uncooked	4 oz. (1 ¼ cups)	2 ¼ cups cooked

Noodles, Spaghetti, uncooked	7 oz.	4 cups cooked
Nuts, chopped	¼ lb.	1 cup
Nuts, Almonds	1 lb.	3 ½ cups
Nuts, Walnuts, broken	1 lb.	3 cups
Nuts, Walnuts, unshelled	1 lb.	1 ½ to 1 ¾ cups
Onion	1 medium	½ cup
Orange	3 – 4 medium	1 cup juice
Raisins	1 lb.	3 ½ cups
Rice, Brown	1 cup	4 cups cooked
Rice, Converted	1 cup	3 ½ cups cooked
Rice, Regular	1 cup	3 cups cooked
Rice, Wild	1 cup	4 cups cooked
Sugar, Brown	1 lb.	2 ½ cups
Sugar, Powdered	1 lb.	3 ½ cups
Sugar, White	1 lb.	2 cups
Vanilla Wafers	22	1 cup fine crumbs
Zwieback, crumbled	4	1 cup

Food Quantities
For Large Servings

	25 Servings	50 Servings	100 Servings

Beverages:

	25 Servings	50 Servings	100 Servings
Coffee	½ lb. and 1 ½ gallons water	1 lb. and 3 gallons water	2 lb. and 6 gallons water
Lemonade	10 – 15 lemons and 1 ½ gallons water	20 – 30 lemons and 3 gallons water	40 – 60 lemons and 6 gallons water
Tea	1/12 lb. and 1 ½ gallons water	1/6 lb. and 3 gallons water	1/3 lb. and 6 gallons water

Desserts:

Layered Cake	1 12" cake	3 10" cakes	6 10" cakes
Sheet Cake	1 10" x 12" cake	1 12" x 20" cake	2 12" x 20" cakes

Watermelon	37 ½ lb.	75 lb.	150 lb.
Whipping Cream	¾ pint	1 ½ to 2 pints	3 – 4 pints

Ice Cream:

Brick	3 ¼ quarts	6 ½ quarts	13 quarts
Bulk	2 ¼ quarts	4 ½ quarts or 1 ¼ gallons	9 quarts or 2 ½ gallons

Meat, Poultry, or Fish:

Fish	13 lb.	25 lb.	50 lb.
Fish, fillets or steaks	7 ½ lb.	15 lb.	30 lb.
Hamburger	9 lb.	18 lb.	35 lb.
Turkey or Chicken	13 lb.	25 to 35 lb.	50 to 75 lb.
Wieners (beef)	6 ½ lb.	13 lb.	25 lb.

Salads or Casseroles:

Baked Beans	¾ gallon	1 ¼ gallons	2 ½ gallons
Jell-o Salad	¾ gallon	1 ¼ gallons	2 ½ gallons
Potato Salad	4 ¼ quarts	2 ¼ gallons	4 ½ gallons
Scalloped Potatoes	4 ½ quarts or 1 12" x 20" pan	9 quarts or 2 ¼ gallons	18 quarts or 4 ½ gallons
Spaghetti	1 ¼ gallons	2 ½ gallons	5 gallons

Sandwiches:

Bread	50 slices or 3 1 lb. loaves	100 slices or 6 1 lb. loaves	200 slices or 12 1 lb. loaves
Butter	½ lb.	1 lb.	2 lb.
Lettuce	1 ½ heads	3 heads	6 heads
Mayonnaise	1 cup	2 cups	4 cups

Mixed Filling:

Meat, Eggs, Fish	1 ½ quarts	3 quarts	6 quarts
Jam, Jelly	1 quart	2 quarts	4 quarts

Microwave Hints

1. Place an open box of hardened brown sugar in the microwave oven with 1 cup of water. Microwave on high for 1 ½ to 2 minutes for ½ lb. or 2 to 3 minutes for 1 lb.

2. Soften hard ice cream by microwaving it at 30% power. One pint will take 15 to 30 seconds; one quart, 30 to 45 seconds; and one-half gallon, 45 to 60 seconds.

3. To melt chocolate, place ½ lb. in glass bowl or measuring cup. Melt uncovered at 50% power for 3 – 4 minutes; stir after 2 minutes.

4. Soften one 8oz. package of cream cheese by microwaving at 30% power for 2 to 2 ½ minutes. One 3oz. package of cream cheese will soften in 1 ½ to 2 minutes.

5. A 4 ½ oz. carton of whipped topping will thaw in 1 minute on the defrost setting. Whipped topping should be slightly firm in the center, but it will blend well when stirred. Do not over thaw!

6. Soften jell-o that has set up too hard – perhaps you were to chill it until slightly thickened and forgot it. Heat on a low power setting for a very short time.

7. Heat hot packs. A wet fingertip towel will take about 25 seconds. It depends on the temperature of the water used to wet the towel.

8. To scald milk, cook 1 cup for 2 to 2 ½ minutes, stirring once each minute.

9. To make dry bread crumbs, cut 6 slices of bread into ½" cubes. Microwave in 3-quart casserole dish for 6 to 7 minutes, or until dry, stirring after 3 minutes. Crush in the blender.

10. Refresh stale potato chips, crackers, or other snacks of such type by putting a plateful in the microwave

for 30 – 45 seconds. Let stand for 1 minute to crisp. Cereals can also be crisped this way.

11. Nuts will be easier to shell if you place 2 cups of nuts in a 1-quart casserole dish with 1 cup water. Cook for 4 to 5 minutes and the nutmeats will slip out whole after cracking the shell.

12. Stamp collectors can place a few drops of water on a stamp to remove it from an envelope. Heat in the microwave for 20 seconds and the stamp will come off.

13. Using a round dish instead of a square one eliminates overcooked corners in baking cakes.

14. Sprinkle a layer of medium, finely chopped walnuts evenly onto the bottom and side of a ring pan or bundt cake pan to enhance the looks and eating quality. Pour in batter and microwave as recipe directs.

15. Do not salt foods on the surface as it causes dehydration and toughens food. Salt after you remove from the oven unless the recipe calls for using salt in the mixture.

16. Heat left-over custard and use it as frosting for a cake.

17. Melt marshmallow cream. Half of a 7oz. jar will melt in 35 – 40 seconds on high. Stir to blend.

18. To toast coconut, spread ½ cup coconut in a pie plate and cook for 3 – 4 minutes, stirring every 30 seconds after 2 minutes. Watch closely, as it quickly browns.

19. To melt crystallized honey, heat uncovered jar on high for 30 – 45 seconds. If jar is large, repeat.

20. One stick of butter or margarine will soften in 1 minute when microwaved at 20% power.

Calorie Counter

Beverages:

Apple Juice, 6oz.	90
Coffee (black)	0
Cola Type, 12oz.	115
Cranberry Juice, 6oz.	115
Ginger Ale, 12oz.	115
Grape Juice, (from frozen concentrate), 6oz.	142
Lemonade, (from frozen concentrate), 6oz.	85
Milk, protein fortified, 1 cup	105
Milk, Skim, 1 cup	90
Milk, Whole, 1 cup	160
Orange Juice, 6oz.	85
Pineapple Juice, unsweetened, 6oz.	95
Root Beer	150
Tonic (quinine water) 12oz.	132

Breads:

Cornbread, 1 small square	130
Dumplings, 1 med.	70
French Toast, 1 slice	135
Melba Toast, 1 slice	25
Muffins, Blueberry, 1 muffin	110
Muffins, Bran, 1 muffin	106
Muffins, Corn, 1 muffin	125
Muffins, English, 1 muffin	280
Pancakes, 1 (4")	60
Pumpernickel, 1 slice	75
Rye, 1 slice	60
Waffle, 1	216
White, 1 slice	60 - 70
Whole Wheat, 1 slice	55 - 65

Cereals:

Cornflakes, 1 cup	105
Cream of Wheat, 1 cup	120
Oatmeal, 1 cup	148
Rice Flakes, 1 cup	105
Shredded Wheat, 1 biscuit	100
Sugar Krisps, ¾ cup	110

Crackers:

Graham, 1 cracker	15 – 30
Rye Crisp, 1 cracker	35
Saltine, 1 cracker	17 – 20
Wheat Thins, 1 cracker	9

Dairy Products:

Butter or Margarine, 1 tbsp.	100
Cheese, American, 1oz.	100
Cheese, Camembert, 1oz.	85
Cheese, Cheddar, 1oz.	115
Cheese, Cottage Cheese, 1oz.	30
Cheese, Mozzarella, 1oz.	90
Cheese, Parmesan, 1oz.	130
Cheese, Ricotta, 1oz.	50
Cheese, Roquefort, 1 oz.	105
Cheese, Swiss, 1 oz.	105
Cream, light, 1 tbsp.	30
Cream, heavy, 1 tbsp.	55
Cream, sour, 1 tbsp.	45
Hot Chocolate, with Milk, 1 cup	277
Milk Chocolate, 1oz.	145 – 155
Yogurt made w/ whole milk, 1 cup	150 – 165
Yogurt made w/ skimmed milk, 1 cup	125

Eggs:

Fried, 1 large	100
Poached or Boiled, 1 large	75 – 80
Scrambled or in Omelet, 1 large	110 - 130

Fish and Seafood:

Bass, 4oz.	105
Salmon, broiled or baked, 3oz.	155
Sardines, canned in oil, 3oz.	170
Trout, fried, 3 ½ oz.	220
Tuna, in oil, 3oz.	170
Tuna, in water, 3oz.	110

Fruits:

Apple, 1 medium	80 – 100
Applesauce, sweetened, ½ cup	90 – 115
Applesauce, unsweetened, ½ cup	50
Banana, 1 medium	85
Blueberries, ½ cup	45
Cantaloupe, ½ cup	24
Cherries (pitted), raw, ½ cup	40
Grapefruit, ½ medium	55
Grapes, ½ cup	35 – 55
Honeydew, ½ cup	55
Mango, 1 medium	90
Orange, 1 medium	65 – 75
Peach, 1 medium	35
Pear, 1 medium	60 – 100
Pineapple, fresh, ½ cup	40
Pineapple, canned in syrup, ½ cup	95
Plum, 1 medium	30
Strawberries, fresh, ½ cup	30

Strawberries, frozen and sweetened, ½ cup	120 – 140
Tangerine, 1 large	39
Watermelon, ½ cup	42

Meat and Poultry:

Beef, Ground (lean), 3oz.	185
Beef, Roast, 3oz.	185
Chicken, broiled, 3oz.	115
Lamb Chop (lean), 3oz.	175 – 200
Steak, Sirloin, 3oz.	175
Steak, Tenderloin, 3oz.	174
Steak, Top Round, 3oz.	162
Turkey, dark meat, 3oz.	175
Turkey, white meat, 3oz.	150
Veal, Cutlet, 3oz.	156
Veal, Roast, 3oz.	76

Nuts:

Almonds, 2 tbsp.	105
Cashews, 2 tbsp.	100
Peanuts, 2 tbsp.	105
Peanut Butter, 1 tbsp.	95
Pecans, 2 tbsp.	95
Pistachios, 2 tbsp.	92
Walnuts, 2 tbsp.	80

Pasta:

Macaroni or Spaghetti, cooked, ¾ cup	115

Salad Dressings:

Blue Cheese, 1 tbsp.	70
French, 1 tbsp.	65
Italian, 1 tbsp.	80
Mayonnaise, 1 tbsp.	100
Olive Oil, 1 tbsp.	124
Russian, 1 tbsp.	70

Salad Oil, 1 tbsp.	120

Soups:

Bean, 1 cup	130 – 180
Beef Noodle, 1 cup	70
Bouillon and Consommé, 1 cup	30
Chicken Noodle, 1 cup	65
Chicken with Rice, 1 cup	50
Minestrone, 1 cup	80 – 150
Split Pea, 1 cup	145 – 170
Tomato with Milk	170
Vegetable	80 - 100

Vegetables:

Asparagus, 1 cup	35
Broccoli, cooked, ½ cup	25
Cabbage, cooked, ½ cup	15 – 20
Carrots, cooked, ½ cup	25 – 30
Cauliflower, ½ cup	10 – 15
Corn (kernels), ½ cup	70
Green Beans, 1 cup	30
Lettuce, shredded, ½ cup	5
Mushrooms, canned, ½ cup	20
Onions, cooked, ½ cup	30
Peas, cooked, ½ cup	60
Potato, baked, 1 medium	90
Potato, chips, 8 – 10	100
Potato, Mashed, w/ milk & butter, 1 cup	200 - 300
Spinach, 1 cup	40
Tomato, raw, 1 medium	25
Tomato, cooked, ½ cup	30

Cooking Terms

Au Gratin: Topped with crumbs and/or cheese and browned in oven or under broiler.

Au Jus: Served in its own juices.

Baste: To moisten foods during cooking with pan drippings or special sauce in order to add flavor and prevent drying.

Bisque: A thick cream soup.

Blanch: To immerse in rapidly boiling water and allowed to cook slightly.

Cream: To soften a fat, especially butter, by beating it at room temperature. Butter and sugar are often creamed together, making a smooth, soft paste.

Crimp: To seal the edges of a two-crust pie either by pinching them at intervals with the fingers or by pressing them together with the tongs of a fork.

Crudités: An assortment of raw vegetables (i.e. carrots, broccoli, celery, mushrooms) that is served as a hors d'oeuvre, often accompanied by a dip.

Degrease: To remove fat from the surface of stews, soups, or stock. It's usually cooled in the refrigerator so that fat hardens and is easily removed.

Dredge: To coat lightly with flour, cornmeal, etc.

Entrée: The main course.

Fold: To incorporate a delicate substance such as whipped cream or beaten egg whites, into another substance without releasing air bubbles. A spatula is used to gently bring part of the mixture from the bottom of the bowl to the top. The process is repeated, while slowly rotating the bowl, until the ingredients are thoroughly blended.

Glaze: To cover with a glossy coating, such as a melted and somewhat diluted jelly for fruit desserts.

Julienne: To cut vegetables, fruits, or cheeses into match-shaped silvers.

Marinate: To allow food to stand in a liquid in order to tenderize or to add flavor.

Meuniere: Dredged with flour and sautéed in butter.

Mince: To chop food into very small pieces.

Parboil: To boil until partially cooked; to blanch. Usually final cooking in a seasoned sauce follows this procedure.

Pare: To remove the outermost skin of a fruit or vegetable.

Poach: To cook gently in hot liquid kept just below the boiling point.

Puree: To mash foods by hand by rubbing through a sieve or food mill, or by whirling in a blender or food processor until perfectly smooth.

Refresh: To run cold water over food that has been parboiled in order to stop the cooking process quickly.

Sauté: To cook and/or brown food in a small quantity of hot shortening.

Scald: To heat to just below the boiling point, when tiny bubbles appear at the edge of the saucepan.

Simmer: To cook in liquid just below the boiling point. The surface of the liquid should be barely moving, broken from time to time by slowly rising bubbles.

Steep: to let food stand in hot liquid in order to extract or to enhance flavor, like tea in hot water or poached fruit in sugar syrup.

Toss: To combine ingredients with a repeated lifting motion.

Whip: To beat rapidly in order to incorporate air and produce expansion, as in heavy cream or egg whites.